佐藤優の「公明党」論

A Transformative Force
The Emergence of Komeito as a Driver of Japanese Politics

佐藤優
Masaru Sato

第三文明社

まえがき

　公明党は、日本政治のなかで決定的に重要な役割を果たしている。二〇一六年十二月十日時点で、衆議院には三十五議席（総議席四百七十五の七％）、参議院には二十五議席（総議席二百四十二の一〇％）を有している。しかし、公明党は国会で占める議席をはるかに超える政治的影響力がある。自公連立政権においても、公明党の政策が色濃く反映するものが多い。その一つが、二〇一五年九月十九日に成立した平和安全法制だ。このとき公明党が「平和の党」の原則を裏切ったというようなことを言う有識者がいたが、それは間違いだ。『公明新聞』のインタビューに答えた私はこう述べた。

――平和安全法制に対する評価は。

佐藤 公明党の主張に沿って評価するならば百点満点だ。公明党は、今回の平和安全法制は、昨年7月1日の閣議決定から一歩も出ていないと言っている。

昨年の閣議決定は、集団的自衛権と個別的自衛権が重なる範囲を明確にしたものだ。これで、なし崩し的に個別的自衛権の解釈を広げて、実は集団的自衛権の範囲に大幅に踏み込んで活動する、といったことはできなくなった。

また、日本の防衛に必要な活動は問題なくできるのだから、憲法9条を改正する必要もなくなった。

一方で、今回の法制度は、人によって異なる解釈ができる余地がある。だから、法整備で終わり、ではなく、いかに昨年の閣議決定の趣旨を守って運用するかが重要になる。

――法制度の運用面で注意すべきことは。

佐藤 例えば今の政権はホルムズ海峡の機雷除去に意欲を示す向きがあったが、それが現実的ではない、との答弁を引き出したのは、14日（編注・二〇一五年九月十四日）の山口那津男代表の委員会質問だ。通常、与党の議員から政権の勇み足をただすような質問が出されることは想定されない。だが、現実に平和を維持するためには、大規模なデモを繰り返すよりも、こうした着実な取り組みで懸念を一つ一つ払しょくしていくことのほうが、よほど力になる。

時に権力者は、実証性と客観性を欠いて、自分が望むように世の中を解釈しようとすることがある。だが、公明党には、人間主義と平和主義の信念に基づく確かなリアリズム（現実主義）と論理の力がある。公明党が今後やらなければならないことは、安全保障上の具体的な問題が出たときに、現実に即して客観的かつ論理的に考え、そして昨年の閣議決定に照らして安保法制を解釈して、平和を守っていくことだ。

——公明党の役割について。

佐藤 昨年からの安全保障論議の中で、公明党の立ち位置は変化している。これまで、公明党は社会福祉、教育などの面で評価されてきたが、昨年からは、安全保障政策の主要な意思決定権者だとは言えなかった。しかし、昨年からは、重要な決定権者の一員になっており、国の中枢に与える影響力がますます強まっている。そこを過小評価しないことが重要だ。

私が理解する限り、公明党は、存在論的平和主義だ。つまり、公明党は、平和を創(つく)るために生まれ、平和を守るために活動し続ける存在だ。公明党は、現実の政治の場で、しっかりとその責務を果たしている。今後もしっかりと公明党を支持していくことが、そのまま現実の平和を維持することにつながる。

民主党は表面上、集団的自衛権に激しく反対しているが、本心では大半の人が集団的自衛権に賛成だ。反対は政局的な観点からだ。公明党は、その人間主

義と平和主義の価値観に基づいて、日本国憲法で認められる個別的自衛権の範囲を超えた、いわゆるフルスペックの集団的自衛権に反対している。だから公明党は信頼できる〉(二〇一五年九月二十五日付『公明新聞』)

ここで私は「存在論的平和主義」という言葉で述べたが、重要なのは、公明党がしっかりした価値観を持った政党であるということだ。そして、その価値観を形成するうえで重要な機能を果たしているのが公明党の支持母体である創価学会だ。本書で詳しく述べたが、一九七〇年代の「言論問題」以後、創価学会と公明党の関係について公(おおやけ)に語ることがタブーのようになってしまった。それに、多くの有識者やマスコミ関係者が、宗教団体が一切政治に関与しないことを政教分離と勘違いしている。この間違えた傾向を正す作業に現在、公明党は鋭意取り組んでいる。二〇一六年に私との共著で山口那津男公明党代表は、〈日本国憲法に定められた「政教分離」の原則は、特定の宗教団体の政治活動

5　まえがき

を縛るものではありません。「国家が特定の宗教を優遇したり排斥(はいせき)してはならない」。これが政教分離の正しい考え方です〉(佐藤優/山口那津男『いま、公明党が考えていること』潮新書、二〇一六年、二三頁)と指摘した。私も山口氏の考えに完全に同意する。

さらに重要なのは、公明党が創立五十周年を迎えた二〇一四年十一月に刊行された公式の文書である『大衆とともに——公明党50年の歩み』において、公明党が池田大作創価学会会長(当時)によって創設された経緯について記したことだ。この本のグラビアの二頁目に池田大作SGI(創価学会インタナショナル)会長の写真が掲げられている。キャプションにはこう記されている。

〈池田大作公明党創立者(創価学会会長=当時)

1962年(昭和37年)9月13日の公明政治連盟(公政連)第1回全国大会(東京・豊島公会堂)で、創立者である池田会長はあいさつのなかで、公明議員の

在り方として、「大衆とともに語り、大衆とともに戦い、大衆の中に死んでいく」との指針を示された。その池田会長の言葉は、2年後の公明党結党に際し、党の根本指針として党綱領に明記された〉

池田氏の「大衆とともに語り、大衆とともに戦い、大衆の中に死んでいく」という指針に基づいて公明党は五十年間闘ってきたのである。今重要なのは、山口代表が指摘した正しい政教分離の価値観に基づいて公明党を理解することだと私は考える。

私は公明党員でも、公明党の支持母体である創価学会のメンバーでもない。日本におけるプロテスタントの最大教派である日本基督教団に所属するキリスト教徒だ。特定の支持政党はない。しかし、私がキリスト教徒であることが、公明党の人々や公明党を支持する創価学会のメンバーと話をするときの障害にはならない。政教分離の精神は公明党に根付いている。平和、生命、人間を尊

重する創価学会と価値観を共有する人々が、政治のプロとして活躍しているので、公明党は信頼できるのである。また、「権力に迎合した」「平和の看板に泥を塗った」と非難されながらも、現実の政治のなかで、「大衆とともに語り、大衆とともに戦い、大衆の中に死んでいく」努力をしている公明党員が好きなのである。

本書で私が意図したことは、『大衆とともに――公明党50年の歩み』を深く読み解くことで、政治を通して確固たる価値観を持つ公明党員が、日本と世界の宿命を大きく転換しているという現実を示すことだ。二十一世紀の日本政治が公明党を中心に展開されていくようになることに期待している。

（二〇一六年十二月十日脱稿）

佐藤　優

佐藤優の「公明党」論　目次

まえがき　1

第一章　日本政治に深く打ち込まれた「杭」　13

第二章　大衆政党としての公明党の本質　33

第三章　「助走期」を終え、「飛翔期」に入った公明党　53

第四章 「言論問題」に真正面から向き合った党史 73

第五章 外交でも重要な役割を果たしてきた公明党 87

第六章 公明党「与党化」の意義を考える 109

本書は、月刊誌『第三文明』に連載された「公明党50年の歩みを読む」(二〇一六年二月号〜七月号)を基に一部加筆修正し、「まえがき」を書き下ろしたものです。

第1章 日本政治に深く打ち込まれた「杭」

公明党を見ていれば日本政治はわかる

今の日本の政治を考え、今後について予測する場合、私が最も強く意識しているのは、公明党と、その支持母体・創価学会の動きだ。むしろ、「公明党と創価学会の動きさえ見ていれば、日本政治の動向はわかる」と言い切ってもよい。

それは一つには、第二次安倍晋三政権以降の政治状況が、自民党だけが強い「一強多弱」の状況に陥っているからである。

二〇一二年の下野以降の民主党は弱体化し、「二大政党制」はもはや存在しない。今や政権に影響を与える「野党」はなく、自民党の暴走を阻止できる現実的な政治勢力は、「与党内野党」といわれることもある公明党しかない。

また、公明党以外の政党は、変化しない「与件」——所与の条件として考えることが可能である。

自民党の方向性も予測できる。共産党の方向性も予測できる。民主党が、物理学でいう「ブラウン運動」（溶媒中の微粒子が不規則に運動する現象）のような状態になってバラバラであることもわかる。旧「維新」系が、彼らにとっては重要でも、日本全体にとっては重要でない抗争に明け暮れていることもわかる。いずれの政党の動きも、日本社会全体の動向を左右するような変化ではなくなっている。今はただ一つ、公明党の動向だけが、日本社会の今後の方向性を決定する要因になり得るのだ。

それは、ただ単に、公明党が人数的に衆院・参院の「キャスティング・ボート」を握っている、というレベルの話ではない。「日本政治の基本的な構造を変え得る政党」が、公明党だけだということだ。

日本には、現実的な政治力を持つ「宗教政党」は公明党しかない。それは言い換えれば、公明党以外の政党は、世俗的な力の範囲内での合従連衡、権力の分配を繰り返しているだけだということだ。

ただ一つ、公明党のみが、世俗を超えた超越的な視点から政治を相対化し、鳥瞰することができる。政治のなかに、「権力の論理」を超えた超越的価値の論理を持ち込むことができる。だからこそ、既成の政治の論理だけでは、公明党の動向を推し量ることはできない。その意味で予見不可能な側面があり、公明党・創価学会の動きを注視する必要があるのだ。

しかも、今回の軽減税率導入をめぐる一連の動きを見てもわかるとおり、安倍政権内における公明党の存在感は着実に高まっている。

自公連立政権誕生（一九九九年）からの長い間、公明党は、自民党の「下駄の雪」だとか、「ギブ・アンド・テイクではなく、自民党にギブばかりしてい

る」などと揶揄されてきた。しかしここにきて、少数の公明党が多数の自民党に大きな譲歩を余儀なくさせるほど、力をつけてきたのである。今後もこの流れは続き、公明党は日本政治の鍵を握る存在であり続けると、私は考える。

そこで、本書では、公明党の存在意義や今後果たすべき役割について、私なりに意見をまとめておきたいと思う。

そのための格好のテキストとな

1964年11月17日の公明党結成大会。「大衆福祉の公明党」「日本の柱公明党」の垂れ幕が見える

るのが、公明党史編纂委員会の手になる『大衆とともに——公明党50年の歩み』(発行・公明党機関紙委員会／以下、『五十年史』と略)だ。二〇一四年十一月に、公明党結党五十年を記念して発刊された公式の党史である。『五十年史』の記述を逐条的に追うのではなく、そのなかのエッセンスを抽出する形で、公明党の歴史と今に迫ってみたい。

大胆にして周到な「はじめに」の文章

『五十年史』で何よりも画期的であるのは、党の創立者である池田大作SGI会長の存在を、しっかりと位置づけている点だ。

と言うと、「創立者を党史のなかにきちんと位置づけるのは、当たり前ではないか」と思う向きもあるだろう。だが、公明党と創価学会の場合、ことはそ

う単純ではなかった。一九七〇年代以降、いわゆる「学会・公明党の政教一致批判」に配慮して、池田氏が創立者であると強調することは避けてきた経緯があるのだ。

たとえば、公明党の公式サイトを見れば、今なお、年表が公明政治連盟（公明党の前身）の結成から始まっていて、その前史である創価学会の政治進出には触れられていない。それは、学会・公明党が世論の集中砲火を浴びたいわゆる「言論問題※1」のダメージによって、「羹に懲りて膾を吹く」ように、過度の配慮をしている姿に見える。

※1　言論問題
政治評論家・藤原弘達が一九六九年に出版した『創価学会を斬る』をめぐって起きた問題。創価学会・公明党に対する、事実に基づかない誹謗中傷が書かれていた同書について、学会側が抗議したことが「言論・出版妨害だ」と騒がれ、創価学会と公明党の関係が「政教一致」であるとの誤解が広がった。

しかし、そうした「過度の政教分離」が、一般国民にある種の「うさんくささ」を感じさせてしまっている。外部から見ると、学会と公明党が互いの関係について「隠そう」としていて、「不誠実である」ように見えてしまうのだ。

だからこそ私は、著書『創価学会と平和主義』(朝日新書)のなかで、「公明党と創価学会はお互いの距離を、外部の人間の目にも見える形で縮めるべきだ」と提言した。

そもそも、諸外国には、ドイツの与党「キリスト教民主同盟（CDU）」など、宗教政党がたくさんある。何しろ、東西ドイツ統一以前の東ドイツ（ドイツ民主共和国）にすら、「キリスト教民主同盟」は存在したのである。無神論の立場を取る社会主義国家にすら宗教政党があったことは、象徴的だ。キリスト教のような「世界観型」の宗教にとって、政治もまた世界の一部であるから、そこだけを切り離して考えることは不可能なのである。

創価学会／日蓮仏法もまた「世界観型の宗教」であるから、政治活動だけを自分たちの生活から切り離すことは、そもそもできないのだ。

ともあれ、宗教団体の政治参加それ自体は、憲法の政教分離原則に何ら抵触するものではない。学会・公明党に対する「政教一致批判」のほうが、「ためにする批判」であり、歪(ゆが)んでいるのだ。

したがって、公明党はもっと堂々と、池田大作氏によって創立されたこと、日蓮仏法の価値観を根底に据えた政党であることを、公(おおやけ)に表明していくべきだというのが、私の考えだ。

しかるに、『五十年史』では、巻頭の口絵（グラビア）の最初の見開きに、創立当時の若き池田氏の写真が一頁を割(さ)いて大きく掲載されている。しかも、口絵に続いて登場する、山口那津男(なつお)・公明党代表の筆になる「はじめに」は、次のような一節で始められている。

「公明党は1964（昭和39）年11月17日に、池田大作創価学会会長（当時）の発意によって結成された。『大衆とともに語り、大衆とともに戦い、大衆の中に死んでいく』（池田大作公明党創立者）の指針のもとで、大衆福祉の実現をめざして、活発に活動を展開し、本年2014（平成26）年11月17日、結党50年の佳節を迎えた」

この最初の一文からして、非常によく練られている印象を受ける。つまり、創価学会会長としての創立であること、「大衆とともに語り、大衆とともに戦い、大衆の中に死んでいく」という方針も、池田大作氏が打ち出したものであること――その二つが明示されているからだ。

それは言い換えれば、今では党の綱領から消えてしまった「王仏冥合」の理念が、この「はじめに」の冒頭でもう一度、「王仏冥合（おうぶつみょうごう）※2」という語は使わずに打ち出されたということでもある。その意味でも、大胆にして慎重に練られ

た一文と言えよう。「はじめに」には、次のような一文もある。

「時代は中道に収斂(しゅうれん)しつつあるというが、何もそれは単に左右の距離が縮まったという意味ではないだろう。冷戦後世界が得た真意は、『国家』とか『イデオロギー』のための個人や人間ではない。人間自身の幸福な生存こそが目的価値なのだ。『国家』『イデオロギー』『資本』、いかなる主義・主張も、機構も制度も、全(すべ)ては人間に奉仕すべき存在だということではなかったか。それが『戦争』と『革命』の世紀といわれた20世紀の総括であり、21世紀への申し送り事項であったはずだ。中道への収斂とは、それが含意(がんい)されていると思う」

この一文が示すものは何か。それは、国家・イデオロギー・資本、いかなる主義・主張、機構・制度よりもさらに高い価値を公明党は志向し、政治活動の

※2　王仏冥合

仏法の生命尊重、慈悲の精神が、あらゆる人間の営み、文化の根底に定着すること。

根底に据えているということだろう。

そして、その「価値」に当たるものとして、「人間自身の幸福な生存こそが目的価値」であると明言されている。人間のなかにこそ、ひいては生命そのもののなかにこそ、何ものにも代えがたい至高の価値がある——これは、「一人の人間の命は地球よりも重い」などという単なるセンチメンタリズムではない。創価学会の「生命論」を根底に据えた、確固たる哲学としての「生命至上主義」「人間主義」から発せられた言葉なのである。

先に引いた一節からして、池田大作氏の「人間主義」の哲学を凝縮したような一文と言える。また、「21世紀への申し送り事項」との言葉は、明らかに池田氏と歴史家アーノルド・トインビーの名高い対談集『二十一世紀への対話』(聖教ワイド文庫)をふまえて用いられている。創立者である池田氏の思想・哲学を、今の公明党も根底に据えているということが、この「はじめに」の一文

のなかに含意されているのだ。

公明党は昔も今も、しばしば「中道政党」と評される。それは、「単純に左翼的でも右翼的でもない」というニュアンスであり、時には「状況しだいで右寄りにも左寄りにもなる、どっちつかずのコウモリ政党」という皮肉を込めて用いられる。

しかし、公明党が志向する「中道」とは、そのように底の浅いものではない。それは、国家やイデオロギーなどの都合に左右されず、常に「人間自身の幸福な生存」をこそブレない軸とするという意味での「中道」なのである。「はじめに」の文章には、「中道」の一語に込めたそのような真意が、簡潔明瞭に表現されている。この文章は山口代表自らが書いたものだと思うが、党創立者の哲学を凝縮した見事な文が書けること自体、山口氏が政治家である以前に一宗教人として、しっかりとした価値観を持っていることを示している。

哲学なき政党は杭のない建物に等しい

『五十年史』の「はじめに」から、もう一つ印象的な一節を引用しよう。

「公明党に対し、『日本政治の命綱』『地中深く打ち込んだ杭』の如き政党と評する政治学者もいる。一時的な『風』や『ブーム』に左右されず、常に一定勢力を維持し、右顧左眄（うこさべん）の人気取りや『迎合（げいごう）』政治とも無縁であり、政治全体が液状化するような状況でも微動だにせず屹立（きつりつ）している党、としての公明党の存在を譬（たと）えてのものだろう」

「地中深く打ち込んだ杭」とは、先に引いた一節の「人間自身の幸福な生存こそが目的価値」との哲学の謂（いい）であろう。公明党は、創立者・池田大作氏の、日蓮仏法をふまえた「人間主義」が、杭のように真っ芯（しん）にまで打ち込まれた政党

なのである。

おりしも日本では、マンション建設における「杭打ちデータ偽装」が、大きな問題になっている。耐震のため、地下の岩盤にまで打ち込まれるはずの杭が、実は岩盤に届いていなかった。にもかかわらず、データを改竄して岩盤に到達したかのように偽装していた、という事件である。

山口代表が『五十年史』の「はじめに」を執筆した時点では、偽装問題は発覚していなかった。したがって、偶然の一致ではあろうが、私は今回「はじめに」を読み直して、杭打ち偽装問題を想起せずにはいられなかった。それだけメタファー（隠喩）として優れているということだろう。

政党を建物にたとえるなら、地中深く、固い岩盤に届くまで打たれた「杭」に当たるのは、政治活動の根幹を成す哲学であろう。しかしながら、その「杭」に当たる確固たる哲学を持っている政党は、日本においては公明党しか

ない（「日本共産党も、共産主義という思想を根幹に据えているではないか」と思う向きもあろうが、共産党と公明党の根本的な相違については、章をあらためて論じる）。
ほかの政党は、表面上は立派な建物に見えても、「杭」たる哲学がない。だからこそ、「一時的な『風』や『ブーム』に左右され」右顧左眄の人気取りや『迎合』政治」に走って、常にフラフラと揺れ動いているのだ。「はじめに」の、「日本政治の命綱」「地中深く打ち込んだ杭」という言葉には、山口代表の強烈な自負が示されているのである。

「過度の政教分離」を正した画期的な書

『五十年史』は、一章を割いて「言論問題」を取り上げ、当時向けられた批判の数々を論破している。また、別の一章では「政教一致批判」を取り上げ、公

明党の政権参加が憲法上何ら問題がないと、堂々と主張している。

これらは、私にとってまさに「わが意を得たり」であった。公明党は創立五十年の節目に当たって、ようやく「過度の政教分離」を正し、池田氏の存在の重要性をきっぱりと表明したのである。その意味で『五十年史』は画期的な書物であり、今後公明党や創価学会について論じるための基本文献の一つになり得るものだと思う。

また、『五十年史』が刊行されてからすでに一年以上がたつが、その内容についての批判（政教一致）とする批判）は、管見の範囲では皆無に等しい。そのこと自体、公明党についての国民の理解が進んできている証左であろうし、これまでの「過度の政教分離」が「羹に懲りて膾を吹く」の類いであったことを示してもいよう。

かつて公明党・創価学会に向けられた「政教一致批判」がもし正当なもので

あったなら、『五十年史』の記述も問題視され、国会の場で取り上げられて公明党批判に使われただろう。そのような動きがなかったこと自体、「政教一致批判」がためにするものであったことの逆証明なのである。

「政教一致批判」がなかったこと以上に、『五十年史』自体に対する世間の反発も、ほとんどなかった。ということは、これまで「過度の政教分離」を続けてきた公明党は、実は「幻影におびえていた」面もあるのではないか。公明党が勇気を持って一歩前に踏み出し、池田氏との密接な関係を明確に可視化する党史を世に問うてみたら、意外にも世間はすんなりと受け入れたのだから……。

公明党が日本政治のメインプレーヤーに

しかし、この『五十年史』のように池田氏の存在を前面に出した党史が、仮

に二十年前に刊行されていたら、どうだっただろう。

公明党創立三十周年に当たる一九九四年といえば、自民党が下野し、公明党は非自民連立内閣（羽田孜内閣）の一角を占めていた時期。そのことで、公明党の与党入りが激しい「政教一致批判」の的になっていたころである。そのなかで池田氏の存在をストレートに出した党史など刊行したら、公明党攻撃の格好の材料となったに違いない。

二十年前なら大騒ぎになっていた内容が、今は何ら問題にならず、世間の反発もない。そうした変化が示すのは、自公連立の十数年間で、日本社会の公明党に対する見方が大きく変わったということである。

二〇一五年の一年だけを見ても、公明党が昔に比べて大きく存在感を増していることは、誰の目にも明らかだろう。春から秋にかけては「平和安全法制」をめぐる論議で、年末にかけては軽減税率導入をめぐる論議で、連日連夜、マ

スメディアに公明党の名が躍らない日はなかったと言ってよい。もちろん、そのなかには公明党への批判も少なくなかったが、ともあれ、安全保障や税制などという国家の根幹をめぐる問題で、公明党が日本政治のメインプレーヤーとなった一年であったことは確かだ。二十年前には考えられなかった事態である。昔は、公明党が「主役」になり得るのは、福祉や教育など特定の領域のみだったのだから……。

世間の見方が変わるとともに、公明党自体も、与党である時期が長くなるにつれ、変わった。その変化を、公明党に批判的な人たちは「与党になって、公明党は変質・堕落（だらく）した」と見なすのだろうが、私はそうは考えない。むしろ、与党入りは公明党に大きな成長をもたらしたと考えている。この点は章をあらためて論じよう。

第2章 大衆政党としての公明党の本質

池田会長の言葉に注目して『五十年史』を読む

前章で、私は『五十年史』は、党の創立者である池田大作氏（SGI会長）の重要性をきちんと位置づけている点が画期的だ〟と述べた。

それは、前回取り上げた「はじめに」の記述に限ったことではない。『五十年史』は、随所に池田氏の発言が取り上げられており、党の歩みを常に創立者が見守ってきたことが読者にも感じられるつくりになっているのだ。

実は、私が持っている『五十年史』は、池田氏の発言が引用された部分を蛍光ラインマーカーでマーキングしてある。パラパラッと開いたとき、池田氏の発言部分だけがすぐ目に入るようになっているのだ。なぜそういうことをするかというと、私が受けてきた神学的訓練に基づく「癖(くせ)」のようなものだ。

海外で刊行されている『聖書』には、イエス・キリストの言葉と伝えられる部分だけがゴシック体になっていたり、赤字になっていたりして、一目瞭然(いちもくりょうぜん)に区別できるようになっているものがある。それにならって、私が文春新書から刊行し、解説も書いた『新約聖書』（全二巻）も、イエスの言葉だけをゴシック体で印刷してある。

最重要人物の発言のみをクローズアップすることによって、本の構造がはっきりと見えてくる。これは、私流の「読書術」である。

私がもし仮に創価学会員向けに『五十年史』をテキストとした読書会を開くとしたら、最初に、「この本に出てくる池田先生の発言部分を、全部ラインマーカーでマーキングしてください」と参加者に伝えるだろう。そして、その部分を中心に勉強していく形にすると思う。

本書においても、随時、池田氏の言葉に注目する形で話を進めていきたい。

「大衆」を代表した初めての政党

『五十年史』では、公明党結党(一九六四年十一月十七日)からの歴史のみならず、その前史に当たる「創価学会文化部」の政治進出、および「公明政治連盟(以下、公政連)」時代についても、一章を割いて綴っている。

公明党の公式サイトの「沿革」が、今なお公政連結成から始まっていることを考えれば、創価学会の政治進出を歴史のなかに明確に位置づけた点でも、『五十年史』は画期的であった。

そして、その第一章「前史」においても、やはり池田大作氏の言葉に大きな比重が置かれている。今や公明党の不滅のスローガンともなった「大衆とともに語り、大衆とともに戦い、大衆の中に死んでいく」の、基になった池田氏の

言葉が長く引用されているのだ。

それは、一九六二年九月十三日に行われた、公政連結成後初の全国大会での来賓あいさつの一節である。

「……最後の最後まで、生涯、政治家として、そして指導者として、大衆に直結していってもらいたい。偉くなったからといって、大衆から遊離して、孤立したり、また組織の上にあぐらをかいたりするような政治家には絶対になっていただきたくないのであります。大衆とともに語り、大衆とともに戦い、大衆のために戦い、大衆の中に入りきって、大衆の中に死んでいっていただきたい。どうか公政連の同志の皆さん方だけは、全民衆のための、大衆のなかの政治家として一生を貫き通していただきたいと、切望するものであります」

この言葉は、「2年後の公明党結党に際し、党の根本指針とすべく、党綱領に明れ、結成大会で発表された」（『五十年史』）。そして、その後半世紀余にわ

たって、公明党の原点として語り継がれてきた。

この「大衆とともに」という言葉について、私なりの見方を書き留めておきたい。「政党」のことを、英語で「Party」という。たとえば、自由民主党は英語では「Liberal Democratic Party」であり、「LDP」と略される。

この「Party」という言葉は、「部分」を意味する「Part」からきている。つまり、政党とは本来、「社会全体の代表」ではなく、社会の「ある部分」の代表なのである。「部分の代表」たる政党が切磋琢磨している状態が、民主政治なのだ。

ところが日本には、公明党の登場以前、庶民大衆という、最もボリュームのある「部分」を代表する政党がなかった。

当時の二大政党は自民党と社会党だが、自民党は〝財界・大企業の代弁者〟となっており、一方の社会党は労働組合中心の政党となっていた。大企業に属

さず、労組にも属さない庶民（たとえば商店主や専業主婦など）を代表する政党はどこにもなく、庶民は「政治の谷間」に放置されていたのだ。

カール・マルクスに、『ルイ・ボナパルトのブリュメール18日』という著作がある（邦訳は岩波文庫、平凡社ライブラリーなど）。フランス皇帝ナポレオン三世のクーデターの成立過程を分析した評論だが、現代日本の政治状況になぞらえて読んでも面白い本だ。

そのなかでマルクスは、〝自分が所属する『部分』を代表する党派が存在しないと、人は自分の利益に反する党派にからめとられてしまう〟という意味のことを書いている。公明党登場以前の日本では、庶民たちがまさにそのような状況に置かれていた。「自分たちの声を代弁してくれる政党がない。それでも、選挙ではどこかの政党に投票せざるを得ない」というジレンマのなかにあったのだ。

そうした政治状況ゆえ、公明党は「あらゆる階層のいっさいの民衆を包含しうる大衆政党」（結成時の党綱領）を目指し、庶民大衆という〝最大の部分〟を代表する初めての政党として登場したのである。

公明党は宗教政党としての強みを発揮すべき

そのような「大衆政党」が、公明党という宗教政党として姿を現した点にも、私は感慨を覚える。

「加入戦術」という言葉がある。新左翼の用語で、自力での組織拡大が難しい場合、まず既成政党や政治団体に参加し、その内側から自分たちの影響力を徐々に広げていくという組織戦術のことである。公明党登場以前、日本の宗教団体が政治に関わるやり方は、基本的にこの「加入戦術」であった。自前の政

党を組織するほどの力がないから、自民党なり別の党なりを応援して、見返りに政治的利益を得るというやり方であったのだ。

現在でも、新宗教の多くはこの「加入戦術」によって政治に関わっている。つまり、「加入戦術」を取らず、自前の政党を持って確固たる政治力を持ち得た宗教政党は、日本には公明党しか存在しないのだ。

もっとも、ほかの宗教団体が政党をつくったとしても、私は興味がない。日蓮仏法に基づく政党であるからこそ、公明党に興味があるのだ。

公明党はあくまで大衆政党であるから、宗教に出自を持つとはいえ、宗教政策のみに力を注ぐわけにはいかない。それは当然のことだが、私は公明党がもっとストレートに「宗教政党らしさ」を発揮してもいいと考えている。

前回、"言論問題"以降の公明党には「過度の政教分離」に走る傾向があった。その傾向が『五十年史』によって修正されたことは好ましい"と書いた。

だからこそ、これからは実際の政治においても、堂々と「宗教政党らしさ」を発揮してほしいと思う。

その一例として、公明党がその気になればすぐにでもできることを、一つ提案しておきたい。

日本のマスメディアでは、世界のカトリック教会を統率する最高位の聖職者（現在は第二百六十六代フランシスコ）について、「ローマ法王」と「ローマ教皇」という表記が混在している。しかし実は、「ローマ法王」という表記は誤訳なのである。「王」という語は世俗世界の「王」を連想させるから教皇にはふさわしくないし、「法王」の「法」はこの場合、仏教における「法（ダルマ）」を意味するから、カトリック教会の最高聖職者にあてはめるのはおかしい。二重の意味で誤訳なのだ。

実際、日本のカトリック教会の中央団体であるカトリック中央協議会は、

「ローマ法王」という表記にかねて不快感を表明している。一九八一年に、当時のローマ教皇ヨハネ・パウロ二世が来日した際には、日本政府に対して「ローマ教皇」という表記への統一を求めた。併せて、東京都千代田区の「ローマ法王庁大使館」(バチカン市国駐日大使館・総領事館)についても、「ローマ教皇庁大使館」への名称変更を要求した。

だが、日本政府側(外務省)は「日本における各国公館の名称変更はクーデターなどによる国名変更時など、特別な場合以外は認められない」として、要求を突っぱねてしまった。

カトリック中央協議会の公式サイトには、この問題について次のように書かれている。

「日本とバチカン(ローマ法王庁、つまりローマ教皇庁)が外交関係を樹立した当時の定訳は『法王』だったため、ローマ教皇庁がその名称で日本政府に申請。

43　第2章　大衆政党としての公明党の本質

そのまま『法王庁大使館』になりました。日本政府に登録した国名は、実際に政変が起きて国名が変わるなどしない限り、変更できないのだそうです」

以来、現在まで「ローマ法王庁大使館」のままであり、NHKも「ローマ法王」という呼称を用い続けている。

私は自分の著作では必ず「ローマ教皇」と表記しているし、一部のメディアは「教皇」の表記を用いるようになってきたが、今なお「ローマ法王」表記のほうが一般的だ。「日本政府に登録した国名は、実際に政変が起きて国名が変わるなどしない限り、変更できない」という外務省側の弁明に、首をかしげた読者も多いことだろう。というのも、二〇一五年四月、南コーカサス地方のグルジア国について、「ジョージア」に呼称変更する法律が成立したからである。

旧グルジアは、別に政変が起きて国名変更がなされたわけではない。大統領

が来日時に安倍首相に直接会って呼称変更を要求するなど、日本政府への働きかけを重ねた結果なのだ。

そのように、国名表記でさえ、政府がその気になればすぐに変えられる。法王から教皇への呼称変更を拒む理由は、本来はないはずだ。本気で変えようとすれば、すぐにでも変えられるのだ。

そこで私の提案だが、公明党が先導して、法王・法王庁の表記を教皇・教皇庁に変更する法律をつくってはどうだろうか？ 変更したところでさしたる不都合はなく、反対する政党があるとも思えない。おそらく、あっさりと成立するだろう。だが、その呼称変更が与える影響は大きい。カトリック世界と日本の関係を、劇的に改善させる力になるだろう。

その法案を提案する際、公明党は「政党として、宗教の内在的論理を尊重したい」と表明するとよいと思う。宗教人の内在的論理をよく理解する公明党に

ふさわしい働きかけとなるはずだ。

呼称変更が実現すれば世界的ニュースになるはずで、公明党の大きなイメージアップにつながる。バチカン市国という国家の要求を外務省が不当にはねつけてきたのを、公明党の力で改善することになるからだ。「公明党は、創価学会の利益になることしかしないわけではなく、宗教全体を尊重している」という印象も与えられるだろう。

公明党が宗教政党としての強み・存在感を発揮するためにも、ぜひ取り組んでほしい、「小さいけれど大きな改革」である。

公明党は「体制内改革」の政党

『五十年史』を読み解くに当たって、併読しておきたい文献として、池田大作

氏の著作『私の履歴書』が挙げられる。

これは、『日本経済新聞』に長期連載されている人気読み物「私の履歴書」に、池田氏が一九七五年に登場した際の内容をまとめたものだ。池田氏の貴重な自伝である。二〇一六年一月に、聖教ワイド文庫で新装刊されたこともあり、未読の人にはぜひ読んでいただきたい重要文献だ。

この『私の履歴書』のなかに、創価学会の政治進出について真正面から触れた文章がある。「権力との戦い」と題された一編である。そのなかで池田氏は、自らが選挙違反容疑で不当逮捕され、後に裁判で無罪が確定した「大阪事件」（一九五七年）について振り返っている。

「大阪事件」について、池田氏は、前年七月の参院選における創価学会文化部の候補者の大勝利（三人が当選）が引き起こした弾圧であったことを示唆している。

「当時、こうして学会の伸長が明らかになると、それを阻止しようとする動きがあったことは確かである。波が大きければ抵抗も大きいという当然の理(ことわり)であろう」

特に、若き日の池田氏が陣頭指揮を執り、新聞が"まさか"が実現」と書いたほどの奇跡的勝利をもたらした大阪地方区での戦い(学会内で「大阪の戦い」として語り継がれている)は、学会の底力を満天下に知らしめるものだった。

だからこそ、池田氏が弾圧のターゲットとされたのだろう。

大阪事件で無罪を勝ち取るまでの経緯を簡潔(かんけつ)に記したうえで、池田氏はこの「権力との戦い」を次のように結んでいる。

「私は心の奥底(おうてい)で、生涯、不当な権力に苦しむ民衆を守り、民衆とともに進もうと決意せざるをえなくなっていった」

ここで文章は終わっているのだが、私は「そのために、私は公明党をつくっ

たのだ」と続くのだと受け止めた。といっのも、この「権力との戦い」には、最初のほうに「公明党は私が創始したのだが、現在は明確に政教分離している。ともかく、日本の民衆のため、福祉政治の実現のために、党の貢献を期待したい」という一節もあるからだ。

「言論問題」から五年後という段階で書かれたこの随筆では、自らと公明党との関係について触れるにも、細心の注意を払う必要があった。ゆえにこのような書き方になっているのだろう。だが、私が

中之島の大阪市中央公会堂で行われた創価学会大阪大会（1957年7月17日）
©Seikyo Shimbun

斟酌するに、これは池田氏が公明党を創立した「思い」が、文底に沈められる形で明かされた重要な文章だと思う。

池田氏は、大阪事件で不当逮捕され、過酷な取り調べを受けて、国家権力の恐ろしさをまざまざと味わった。そこで「権力との戦い」をあらためて決意したわけだが、そのとき「反権力闘争」の方向に走らなかったことが、池田氏の指導者としての卓越した資質を示している。

国家を否定したり、国家公務員である検察官や裁判官、官僚などを否定してみても、何の意味もない。それでは、権力をやみくもに敵視するだけの青くさい反権力主義に陥ってしまう。池田氏はそうならなかった。氏は、国家権力を打ち倒すべき対象とは見なさず、公明党を反体制政党にもしなかったのだ。

大阪事件に際して、池田氏はおそらく、〝今はまだ、国家権力も創価学会のことを知らなすぎる。そこから大きな齟齬が生じている。もっと、学会につい

て知らしめないといけない"と考えたのではないだろうか。

ならば、どうすればよいか？　国家権力の内側に「同志」をつくっていけばよい。それも、オルグ（勧誘してメンバーに引き入れること）して「同志」を増やしていくなどというやり方ではなく、価値観を共有する学会員を国家権力側に増やしていけばいい。それには時間がかかるが、百年もかかるわけではない。二十五年もあれば成し遂げられることだ。そして、体制の内側から国家を改革していけばよい——若き日の池田氏はそう考えたのだと、私は推察している。

そして、それから六十年近くが過ぎた今、学会員の官僚・法曹・政治家が陸続と生まれ、公明党は与党の重要な一角を占めるに至った。それは、一昔前の週刊誌が書き立てたような、「創価学会の日本支配計画」などという与太話（よたばなし）ではない。「国家権力の内側からの人間を通じた国家改革」、言い換えれば「国家権力の危険性の脱構築」という壮大な人間革命を目指すものであり、

のだ。
　公明党は、結党当初からそのような「体制内改革」を志向していたのであり、近年の与党化も必然であった。『私の履歴書』の「権力との戦い」を読んだうえで『五十年史』を読むと、すべての章がいっそう深く理解できるはずだ。

第3章 「助走期」を終え、「飛翔期」に入った公明党

公明党はもはや「下駄の雪」ではない

　第一章で、私は「安倍政権内における公明党の存在感は着実に高まっている」「(二〇一五年は)公明党が日本政治のメインプレーヤーとなった一年であった」と書いた。そのことについて、今回はもう少し掘り下げて考えてみよう。
　「最近、霞が関の官僚たちが、公明党の国会議員回りの回数を増やしている」という話を耳にした。官僚たちは、公明党がここ一、二年で大きく力をつけてきたことをよく理解しているのだ。
　従来の公明党は、福祉の世界では「向かうところ敵なし」の政党であった。
　しかし、安全保障政策や税制といった国家の根幹を成す分野については、自公連立政権誕生後も、いわば「自民党の専管事項」のようなもので、公明党の影

響力は限定的だった。

だが、数年前から、その図式が大きく崩れてきた。安全保障政策や税制についても、公明党が主役となり、自民党と堂々と渡り合うようになってきたのだ。

軽減税率導入をめぐる攻防は、象徴的だった。当初、軽減税率の食料品への適用範囲について、自民党と財務省は生鮮食品に限るという案を提示していた。それに対して、公明党は「加工食品も含めるべきだ」と主張し、最終的にはその主張が実現したのだ。また、協議の過程では、自民党と財務省が出してきた、「マイナンバーを利用して、軽減分を後日還付（かんぷ）する」というアイデアに公明党が真っ向から異を唱え、引っ込めさせた。

軽減税率導入の細部については、自民党も安倍晋三首相も公明党の意向をほぼ丸のみした決定をしたのである。一連の経緯について、「公明党が財務省の聖域に手を突っ込んだ」と表現したマスコミもあった。確かに、十年前ならあ

り得ないことだったと思う。

そのような日本政治の大きな転換が、ここ一、二年で起きてきた。言い換えれば、公明党が大きく力をつけてきたということだ。それは、グラフを一目盛りずつ上がるような漸進的変化ではなく、階段を駆け上がるような急速な変化であった。

私がその変化をしみじみと実感したのは、二〇一五年九月十四日の参院平和安全法制特別委員会における、公明党の山口（那津男）代表の質問をテレビ中継で見たときであった。そのとき、山口代表は質問のなかで、安倍首相から「ホルムズ海峡への掃海艇派遣は行わない」とする言質を取ったのである。

中東・ペルシャ湾のホルムズ海峡における機雷掃海（除去）活動といえば、安倍首相がかねて、自衛隊派遣による集団的自衛権行使の唯一の具体例として挙げていたものである。それについて、山口代表は質問のなかで理詰めで安倍

首相を追いつめ、「今現在の国際情勢に照らせば、現実問題として発生することを具体的に想定しているものではない」との発言を引き出した。国会という場でそう明言したことによって、安倍首相は、ホルムズ海峡への掃海艇派遣を完全に断念せざるを得なくなったのである。

　与党質問によってそのような転換がなされたことは、これまでに例がないはずだ。要するに、国際法や国際政治に関する知識において、公明党代表が

参院平和安全法制特別委員会で質問する公明党・山口那津男代表（2015 年 9 月 14 日）

自民党総裁を完全に凌駕していたのである。これも、一昔前なら考えられなかったことだと思う。

この事例が象徴的に示すように、自公連立を組んだ初期の段階と現在では、政権内で公明党の持つ「力」が大きく変わったのである。今の公明党は、もはや自民党にしがみついている「下駄の雪」ではなくなっているのだ。にもかかわらず、いまだに「下駄の雪」的イメージで公明党を見ていたら、日本の政治状況を見誤ることになるだろう。

将来、公明党首班政権が必ず誕生する

二〇一四年の結党五十年までの公明党は、長い「助走期」にあったと見ることもできるだろう。その助走期を終え、公明党は二〇一五年から、いよいよ本

格的な「飛翔期」という新しいステージに入ったのだ。

結党から五十年が過ぎ、その間着々と階段を上がってきた公明党が今、一つの「踊り場」のようなところにさしかかっている。『五十年史』は、そのことを無意識のなかで感じ取った公明党の人々がつくった画期的な党史なのだ。

日本の有識者たちのなかにも、公明党がここ一、二年で飛翔期に入ったことを、直観的に見抜いている人は多いのだと思う。だからこそ、公明党を支持する識者は増えてきている。マスコミと深く接する一人として、私はその変化を肌で感じている。

と言うと、「平和安全法制への対応をめぐって、公明党批判がマスコミにあふれたではないか」と思う向きもあるだろう。だが、平和安全法制をめぐる公明党批判の多くは、一昔前のような〝政策の内容以前の批判中傷〟ではなかった。「公明党が自衛隊海外派遣の条件として提示した三原則が、本当に集団的

自衛権行使の歯止めになるのか、疑問だ」などという、ごく普通の政策批判であった。公明党を単に揶揄するのではなく、まともに扱う批判であったのだ。そのことにも、公明党に対する見方が変わってきたことが象徴されている。

私は常々、「創価学会に唯一問題があるとすれば、自らの力の過小評価である」と述べてきた。それは、公明党についても言えることである。公明党は、半世紀にわたって少しずつ蓄えてきた自分たちの力に、もっと自信を持ってよいと思う。

私は、公明党の次の五十年——すなわち結党百年を迎えるまでの間に、公明党首班政権ができると考えている。つまり、公明党のなかから総理大臣が生まれる日が来るのだ。

今の段階でそのようなことを言うと一笑に付されるかもしれない。しかし、単なる夢想の類いではなく、長年日本の政治を観察してきた私の「直観」とし

て、公明党首班政権は将来必ず実現すると思う。

そして、これは私が勝手に推察することだが、山口代表は、将来訪れる公明党首班政権の時代を心のなかで確信し、しっかりと見据えているのではないか。だからこそ、『五十年史』には、来るべきその日のための準備としてつくられた側面がある、と私には思えるのだ。

たとえば、「言論問題」や「政教一致批判」について、『五十年史』ではそれぞれ一章を割いて取り上げ、公明党側に何ら瑕疵がなく、憲法上も問題がないと堂々と主張している。それは、公明党にとっていまだに「のどに刺さった小骨」のような存在になっている二つの問題について、現段階できちんと整理しておき、公明党首班政権の時代に邪魔にならないようにしようとの配慮ではないだろうか。

また、これまで繰り返し述べてきたように、『五十年史』は党創立者の池田

大作SGI会長の貢献をきちんと位置づけた点で画期的な書物なのだが、それは、"言論問題に端を発した「過度の政教分離」を、私の代で正しておきたい"という、山口代表の強い意志によってなされた構成なのではないか。

『五十年史』の刊行は二〇一四年十一月だが、くしくも同じ月に、支持母体の創価学会は重要な「会則の教義条項の改正」を発表した。改正の詳しい中身についてはここでは割愛(かつあい)するが、要は、日蓮正宗との完全な訣別(けつべつ)を宣言するものであった。

私は、『五十年史』の刊行と教義条項改正が同時期に起きたというのは、決して偶然ではないと思う。それは、いわばコインの表裏の関係にある出来事なのである。学会の世界宗教への飛翔の契機となるのが教義条項改正であり、公明党が「助走期」を終えて「飛翔期」に入ったことを示すのが『五十年史』の刊行であるからだ。とはいえ、学会本部と公明党が示し合わせて二つを同時に

行ったということではない。これは「集合無意識」における一致だと思う。

公明党と共産党の本質的差異とは

平和安全法制をめぐって自公政権に対する批判が高まった時期、その批判の受け皿としていわば「漁夫の利」を得たのが、日本共産党である。

そして、共産党もある意味では日本政治の「プレーヤー」になりつつあるし、地方議会でも国会においても衆参両院で今や「野党第二党」になりつつある。怖いことだと思う。

共産党が最近打ち上げている、"安保関連法の廃止を求める野党連立政権"──「国民連合政府」構想というものがある。これは、もともとは社会党（現・社民党）のワーディング（言い回し）「国民連合政権」を借用したものだ。共産

党は従来、「民主連合政府」という言い方をしていたのである。昔の社会党の用語すら〝借用〟して、共産党は日本政治の主要プレーヤーになろうと躍起になっているのだ。

二〇一六年一月四日には、志位和夫委員長ら、共産党の議員たちが通常国会の開会式に出席した。これは、実に六十九年ぶりの出席であった。開会式が天皇陛下を迎えて開催されることについて、天皇制を批判する共産党は「憲法の天皇の『国事行為』から逸脱する」として、一九四七年以降は出席していなかったのだ。突如、その方針を転換したのである。

おそらく、共産党議員たちの集合無意識のなかには、公明党が日本政治の主役となったことへの焦りがあるのだろう。その焦りが、国民の共産党アレルギー払拭のため、なりふり構わぬ融和・協調路線に走るという行動となって表れているのだ。

そもそも、なぜ共産党は公明党に激しい対抗意識を燃やしてきたのだろうか。

それは、本質的な次元から考えれば、共産党は「共産主義という名の宗教」を奉ずる宗教政党だからである。歴史家アーノルド・トインビーも、共産主義を変種の宗教ととらえていた。

ただし、当の共産党員たちは、共産主義を宗教であるなどとは思っておらず、普遍的な科学であると考えている。そして、「宗教は民衆のアヘンである」というマルクスの考えに沿って、むしろ宗教を蔑視している面がある。だからこそ、いっそうタチが悪いのだ。

キリスト教においては、「原罪説」（アダムとイブがエデンの園で犯した神に対する罪が、人間の本性を損ねてしまったとする思想）が、信徒たちが自らを律する重要な「歯止め」の役割を果たしている。つまり、「自分たちが絶対正しい」という唯我独尊に陥らないための歯止めとなるのだ。

創価学会の場合、「原罪」に当たる考え方はないが、師弟不二の思想、師匠との誓いというものが、信徒が自らを律する歯止めとなっているのだろう。それに対して、"宗教としての共産主義"には歯止めがない。だからこそ、どこまでも唯我独尊で突き進んでしまう怖さがある。

二十世紀を代表するキリスト教神学者の一人であるディートリッヒ・ボンヘッファーの、「究極的なるものと究極以前のもの」という概念がある。この概念をふまえて考えると、公明党と共産党の本質的な差異が理解できる。共産党にとっては、政治が「究極的なるもの」である。しかし、公明党にとって政治は「究極以前のもの」である。そこが、両党のいちばん根本的な違いなのだ。

公明党にとって、ひいては創価学会員にとって、政治も学問も仕事も「究極以前のもの」である。「究極的なるもの」は、宗教的真実のなかにあるのだ。

政治が究極ではないからこそ、公明党は政治において、妥協すべきときに適切に妥協できる。「妥協」と言うと、よいイメージではないかもしれない。だが、ドイツの鉄血宰相ビスマルクに「政治とは妥協の産物であり、可能性の芸術である」という名高い言葉があるとおり、妥協は政治に不可欠である。妥協すべきときに妥協できることが、政治家の最重要の資質とも言えるのである。

だが、共産党にとっては政治が究極であり、政治自体が目的になってしまっている。だからこそ、彼らには柔軟な妥協ができない。「何でも反対」のその姿勢は、彼らが適切な妥協ができない政党であることを示している。

弱者目線に立った軽減税率導入

この場を借りて、公明党の軽減税率導入への取り組みについての私見を述べ

ておきたい。

 軽減税率について批判的な政党や有識者のなかには、現金給付と所得税などの払い戻しを組み合わせた「給付付き税額控除」のほうがいい、と主張する人たちがいる。「軽減税率では高額所得者にもある程度恩恵があるのに対して、給付付き税額控除なら低所得者に的を絞った対策ができる」との主張である。一見もっともらしい。だが、私はこれは低所得者層のことを考えていない主張だと思う。

 低所得者層のなかには、"生活習慣弱者"ともいうべき人たちが、かなりの割合で存在する。「生活習慣弱者」とは私の造語で、「健全な生活習慣を持てないがゆえに、低所得などの弱い立場に立たされている人」のことを指す。

 たとえば、毎月の収入を一カ月の生活にきちんと割り振って使えない人たちがいる。賃金が入ったらすぐに使ってしまい、次の給料日まで持たせることが

できず、借金で穴埋めする自転車操業の生活を続ける人たちだ。それが「生活習慣弱者」の一典型であり、だからこそ、その人たちは低所得者層から抜け出せないのだ。

　仮に、一部の政党が主張する「給付付き税額控除」を取り入れたとしたら、毎月支給ではなく、三カ月に一度の支給などという形を取るはずだ。行政の事務処理負担を軽減するためには、そうせざるを得ないからである。

　すると、三カ月に一度、三カ月分の給付が低所得者層に対してなされることになる。そのとき、低所得者層の一定の部分を占める「生活習慣弱者」は、三カ月分を一度に使い果たしてしまうだろう。だからといって、再給付が行われるはずもない。「すぐに使いきってしまったのは、あなたの自己責任です」ということになるのだ。「給付付き税額控除のほうが、低所得者対策として優れている」という主張は、そのような低所得者層の生活実態をまったく考えていない

ない人の発想である。

 それよりは、毎日の食品などの買い物のなかで少しずつ軽減する形にしたほうが、現実的な低所得者対策になる。党の長い歴史のなかで、庶民の生活に常に目を向け、一貫して福祉に力を入れてきた公明党には、そのことがよくわかっていたのだ。軽減税率をめぐる論争のなかで、真に弱者の目線に立っていたのは公明党だったと思う。

 また、二〇一七年四月の消費税引き上げと同時に導入される軽減税率については、「たかが二％(消費税一〇％／軽減税率八％)ではないか」と軽んずる声もある(政府は一六年六月に、消費税増税を一九年十月に延期すると決定した)。
 私は、将来を見据えて考えれば、「たかが」などとは決して言えないと思う。しかしヨーロッパの消費税先進国の事例を見ても、少子高齢化が世界一の速さで進行する日本の現状を見ても、消費税が一〇％にとどまり続けることは考えにく

い。やがて一五％になり、二〇％になる可能性が高いのである。そうした将来のために、今の時点で軽減税率という「枠をつくっておく」こと自体が、非常に重要だったのだ。

軽減税率の対象が食品全般に広がったのも、一〇％引き上げと同時に導入されることになったのも、公明党の手柄である。そしてその手柄は、消費税がさらに引き上げられる将来において、いっそう光彩を放つに違いない。

また、軽減税率に対応する経理方式として、二〇二三年度から「インボイス（適格請求書）制度」の導入が決定したことについて、「中小・零細業者、個人事業主にとっては大きな負担となる」と反対する声がある。だが、私はその意見に与（くみ）しない。

むしろ、日本での消費税導入から三十年近くがたつのに、これまでインボイスが導入されていなかったことのほうが問題だ。それは、「大福帳（だいふくちょう）（江戸・明

治期の商家で用いられた簡便な帳簿）程度のどんぶり勘定にしておいてやるから、お上(かみ)の言うとおりに税を払え」と、国が国民に対して言っているようなものだ。近代国家の発想ではない。

　二十一世紀なのだから、企業なら大福帳ではなく複式簿記できちんと帳簿をつけるのが当たり前だ。今は簡便な会計ソフトも市販されているし、インボイス導入までの移行期間ももうけられているので、決して無理な要求ではない。これを機に、零細企業主もきちんと帳簿のつけ方を覚えたほうが、結局は自分のためにもなるだろう。

　ともあれ、軽減税率の問題にしろ、平和安全法制の問題にしろ、公明党が結党五十年を過ぎていよいよ本格的な「与党化」をしていくに当たっての、乗り越えねばならないハードルのようなものだったと思う。そして、公明党は見事に二つのハードルを乗り越えたのである。

第4章 「言論問題」に真正面から向き合った党史

「過度の政教分離」是正に本気で取り組む公明党

本書では、『五十年史』の特に画期的な点として、①党創立者である池田SGI会長の貢献をきちんと位置づけたこと ②「言論問題」と「政教一致批判」に真正面から向き合ったこと――の二点を挙げてきた。

そして、その二点には密接な関係がある。過去四十数年にわたり、公明党は創価学会との関係について、党の公刊物で池田SGI会長が創立者であることに触れないなど、私が「過度の政教分離」と呼ぶ神経質すぎる対応を取ってきた。それは「言論問題」において、創価学会と公明党がマスコミ・政界から集中砲火的な批判を浴びたことの、いわば〝後遺症〟であった。

「過度の政教分離」は、創価学会員ではない人々から見ると、「公明党が創価

学会との関係を隠そうとしている」かのようないた。つまり、公明党のイメージを大きく毀損していたマイナスポイントであったのだ。

私はそう考えるからこそ、二〇一四年に上梓した拙著『創価学会と平和主義』のなかで、"うさんくさい"と政教分離をめぐる攻防」という一章をもうけ、「公明党と創価学会はお互いの距離を、外部の人間の目にも見える形で縮めるべきだ」と提言した。

だからこそ、その直後に刊行された『五十年史』が、巻頭の口絵に若き日の池田会長の写真を載せ、「はじめに」を「公明党は1964（昭和39）年11月17日に、池田大作創価学会会長（当時）の発意によって結成された」との一文で始めていたことに、快哉を叫んだものだ。

そして、"外部から見た創価学会と公明党の距離"を縮めようとするこうし

た試みは、「言論問題」「政教一致批判」と真正面から向き合うこととセットでなされなければならなかった。「言論問題」こそ「過度の政教分離」を生んだ最大の原因なのだから、そこから目をそらしたまま「過度の政教分離」を正すわけにはいかなかったからだ。

仮に、『五十年史』が口絵と「まえがき」で池田会長について言及しながら、本文で「言論問題」や「政教一致批判」にまったく触れなかったなら、どうだったろうか。

実際、公明党の公式サイトのコンテンツ「写真で読む公明党の50年」を見ると、創価学会文化部による政治進出が最初の項目になっているものの、「言論問題」や「政教一致批判」についての項目はないし、文中でもまったく言及されていない。公明党にとって、"言論問題」や「政教一致批判」にはなるべく触れない"というスタンスのほうが、過去四十数年来のスタンダードであった

76

のだと思う。

　しかし、今後長きにわたって公明党を論ずるための基本文献となるだろう『五十年史』で、「言論問題」「政教一致批判」に言及しなかったなら、将来に禍根(かこん)を残しただろう。また、本全体が中途半端で説得力のないものになってしまっただろう。

　『五十年史』は、そうならなかった。同書は第6章 "開かれた国民政党" 路線──批判吹き荒れた言論問題」で一章を割(さ)いて「言論問題」に言及し、第14章「公明の政権参加、憲法上問題なし」でやはり一章を割いて「政教一致批判」を論破しているのだ。

　この二つの章があることによって、『五十年史』の党史としての価値は格段に上がったと言える。

　まもなく、公明党の山口那津男(なつお)代表と私の対談集『いま、公明党が考えて

いること』が刊行される(二〇一六年四月発刊、潮出版社)。同書で山口代表は、全体の四分の一ほどの分量を割いて、自らの信仰、宗教的信念について堂々と語っている。参院選前の時期に、党代表が創価学会員であることをオープンに語る本を刊行するのは画期的であり、今の公明党が「過度の政教分離」是正に本気で取り組んでいることが、ひしひしと感じられる。そして、そのような動きはまさに『五十年史』から始まったのである。

そもそも、一部マスコミなどが、公明党議員が信仰を持っていることを問題視してきたこと自体がおかしかったのだ。そこには、歪んだ政教分離観に基づく偏見があった。

たとえば、ドイツのアンゲラ・メルケル首相は「キリスト教民主同盟」(CDU)の党首であり、自らの信仰についてマスコミなどでオープンに語ることもある。また、同じくドイツの大統領であるヨアヒム・ガウクに至っては、

「ドイツ福音主義教会」の牧師でもある。だからといって、ドイツでは彼らの信仰が問題視されることなどないのだ。

「言論問題」の経緯と本質を若い学会員も知るべき

私は最近、創価学会員の方と話をする機会が少なくない。そうした機会に驚かされるのは、「言論問題」についてよく知らない若い学会員が、非常に多いことだ。それは、ある意味で無理もない。何しろ、「言論問題」が起きたのは今から四十数年も前なのだから。

だが、「言論問題」は公明党にとっても創価学会にとっても重大な出来事であり、今なお学会・公明党のネガティブなイメージの一因にもなっているのだから、若い学会員もことの経緯と本質について知っておくべきだろう。その意

味でも、『五十年史』が「言論問題」に一章を割いたことの意義は大きい。

なお、「言論問題」について、私は松岡幹夫氏との対談集『創価学会を語る』(第三文明社)のなかで、一章を割いて自らの見解を語っている。なので、詳しくはそちらを読んでいただきたいが、ここでも要点にだけは触れておこう。

「言論問題」とは、一九六九年に政治評論家の藤原弘達氏が、『創価学会を斬る』という本を出版するに当たり、学会側が著者の藤原氏に対して「事実ではない中傷をするのはやめてほしい」と要望をしたことを指す。そのことが「言論・出版の自由」を侵した「弾圧」に当たると見なされ、国会やマスコミを巻き込んだ騒動に発展していったのだ。ちなみに、「言論問題」は学会・公明党側からの呼称であり、一般には「言論・出版妨害事件」の名で知られている。

『創価学会を斬る』の刊行は六九年十一月だが、同年八月末には刊行を予告する電車の中づり広告が大々的に打たれた。この年の十二月には衆議院の解散・

総選挙が行われたが、夏ごろから「年内解散必至」といわれていた状況であった。つまり、藤原氏の本は明らかに同年の衆院選での選挙妨害を意図したものであった。

そのような経緯から、学会側は発刊前に藤原氏との話し合いを行い、出版業務に携わる学会員が取次会社や書店を回って同書の取り扱いに配慮を求めるなど、抗議行動を起こした。それが後に「弾圧」であると批判を浴びたのだが、私は「弾圧」には当たらないと思う。「弾圧」とは、統治者や国家機関（国営メディアなど）によって行われるものである。創価学会は民間団体なのだから、「弾圧」という言葉を用いること自体がおかしい。

また、学会側は要望や抗議行動を行うに当たって、暴力や脅迫を用いたわけではなく、違法なことは一切していない。一民間団体が、自分たちに対する誹謗中傷の書物が刊行されると予告されたとき、「事実でない中傷はやめてほし

い」と、当然の要望をしただけである。それは学会側にとっては、「会員たちにつらい思いをさせたくない。いらざる偏見にさらしたくない」という思いに発した行動であった。

しかも、『創価学会を斬る』はその内容も、ヘイトスピーチ的な誹謗中傷に満ちたひどいものだった。創価学会をナチス呼ばわりし、「日本全体を毒するバイキン」「民主主義の『ドブさらい』」「狂信者の群れ」などという言葉で貶（おと）めていたのだ。つまり、「言論の暴力」の被害者は、むしろ創価学会のほうだったのだ。

にもかかわらず、「言論問題」は学会・公明党を攻撃する格好の材料として、大々的に政治利用された。そして今なお、学会・公明党のネガティブな問題として語られ続けている。だからこそ、公明党が『五十年史』でようやく「言論問題」のマイナス・イメージ克服に挑戦したことは、正しい方向性だと思う。

「戦術的退却」の見本のような池田会長の講演

『五十年史』は、「言論問題」を取り上げた章で、問題の経緯を詳しく説明している。そしてそのなかで、創価学会・公明党が「言論の暴力」の被害者であったという本質を、見事に浮き彫りにしている。

なお、一九七〇年五月三日の創価学会本部総会において、池田会長(当時)は講演のなかで「言論問題」について長く言及した。それは、一連の問題で日本中に吹き荒れた創価学会批判に、会長自らが答え、釈明する内容であった。

池田氏はこのとき、「創価学会はむしろ被害者だ」と突っぱねることもできただろう。しかし、世論の動きをふまえ、苦渋(くじゅう)の選択として謝罪の講演を行い、「戦術的退却」をする道を選んだのである。

その主要部分が『五十年史』にも掲載されているが、今読んでも実に見事な内容である。以下、一部を引用する。

「言論妨害というような陰険な意図は全くなかったが、結果として、これらの言動が全て言論妨害と受け取られ、関係者の方々に圧力を感じさせ、世間にも迷惑をおかけしてしまったことは誠に申し訳なく、残念でならない」

「創価学会と公明党の関係は、あくまでも制度の上で明確に分離していくとの原則を更に貫いていきたい。（中略）むろん創価学会も支持母体として従来通り地域ごとの応援は当然していきたい」

「……見てのとおり、「謝罪」をしたうえで、"学会側に言論妨害という意図はまったくなく、受け取る側の問題にすぎなかった"ことが明確に述べられている。

また、「――原則を更に貫いていきたい」との言葉で、"これまでも政教分

離はなされていたのであり、創価学会の公明党支援には何ら憲法上の問題はない〟ことが示されている。そのうえで、"公明党支援は今後も「従来通り」行っていく〟と、明確に宣言している。

つまり、池田氏はこのとき、レトリックの力を駆使して、言うべきことを過不足なくきちんと言ってみせたのだ。「戦術的退却」の見本のような講演と言えよう。

池田氏のこれまでの歩みを振り返ると、「一度は戦術的退却をするものの、態勢を立て直して二度目に勝利する」というパターンがたびたびあることに気づく。たとえば、池田氏が不当逮捕された「大阪事件」においては、検察側との力関係を冷静に考慮したうえで、一度は容疑を認めるかのような供述をしたことが、戦術的退却に当たる。しかし、「二度目の戦い」である法廷闘争で、見事に無罪を勝ち取った。宗門事件もしかり。一度目の第一次宗門事件では会

長辞任という形で戦術的退却をしたが、第二次宗門事件では宗門に勝利して訣別を果たした。

「言論問題」についてだけは、明確な「二度目の勝利」は訪れていなかった。

しかし、『五十年史』が「言論問題」を真正面から取り上げ、〝われわれこそが「言論の暴力」の被害者だったのだ〟と主張することによって、公明党は長年の懸案事項に決着をつけようとした。当時は学会に対する世間の偏見があまりに強く、戦術的退却をせざるを得なかったが、四十数年を経て学会・公明党への理解も進み、決着できるだけの土壌が整ったのだ。

そして、『五十年史』における「言論問題」の記述について、政界やマスコミからの表立った批判は皆無に等しい。そのことによって、ようやく池田氏にとっての「二度目の勝利」が訪れたのだと、私は思う。

86

第5章 外交でも重要な役割を果たしてきた公明党

外交重視の姿勢を強める公明党

　今夏（二〇一六年）の参議院議員選挙で公明党の福岡選挙区予定候補となっている高瀬ひろみ氏は、元外交官である。また、同じく参院選を戦う大阪選挙区の現職、二期目の石川博崇氏も外務省出身で、中東外交専門の外交官であった（七月十日投開票、両氏ともに当選）。そのように、公明党の若手議員・候補に「外交のプロ」が目立つことは、決して偶然ではないだろう。公明党が、外交を極めて重視していることの反映なのだと思う。
　今の公明党が外交を重視するのは、もちろん一つには世界平和を重視するゆえだが、もう一つには、支持母体の創価学会がいよいよ世界宗教化してきたからだ。

ここ一、二年、『聖教新聞』（創価学会機関紙）では、海外のSGIメンバーの体験談が大きく扱われることが増えた。また、最高指導者である池田大作氏につける紙面の肩書も、かつては「名誉会長」がメインであったが、今では「SGI会長」のほうがメインになっている（その後二〇一六年十一月の会則改正に伴い、三代会長の敬称は、「先生」となっている）。いずれも、世界宗教としての飛翔期に入ったがゆえの変化であろうと思う。

そのように、「創価学会の世界宗教化」のプロセスが進めば進むほど、公明党の役割もよりグローバルなものに変化していく。その変化の一つの表れが、公明党の外交重視の姿勢なのだと思う。

一般に公明党と言えば、「福祉や教育に力を入れてきた政党」という印象が強い。逆に、「外交に力を入れてきた政党」というイメージは強くないかもしれない。「福祉の公明党」とは呼ばれても、「外交の公明党」と呼ぶ人はあまり

いないだろう。

そもそも、公明党から外務大臣が誕生したことは、これまでのところない。だが、外交は外相や首相だけが扱う事柄ではない。公明党は五十年を超える歴史のなかで、党としての取り組みによって日本の外交に重要な役割を果たしてきた。そして、自民党との連立で与党となって以降、その役割の重みはいっそう増している。

今回は、『五十年史』を読み解くことを通じて、公明党の外交に光を当ててみよう。

公明党抜きに日本外交は語れない時代

本書の第一章で、私は「公明党と創価学会の動きさえ見ていれば、日本政治

の動向はわかる」と書いた。それは、外交についてもしかりである。日本外交は、もはや公明党と創価学会の動きを抜きにしては論じられないのだ。

といっても、それは何ら難しいことではない。『公明新聞』と『聖教新聞』をきちんと読んでいればよいのだから……。問題は、その程度の労力すら惜しみながら、公明党について論じようとする半可通の論者がはびこっていることだ。

ちなみに、私は『創価学会と平和主義』を執筆するに当たっても、書籍などの公開情報のみをソース（情報源）とした。しかも、内容の大半は、「セイキョウオンライン」（『聖教新聞』のネット版）や創価学会公式サイト（SOKAnet）で読める記事を資料としていた。それはなぜかというと、検証可能性を担保しておくためである。「佐藤優はこう書いているが、本当だろうか？」と思った読者は、ネットで検索すれば資料として用いた当該記事が読める。そのことが重

要なのだ。

世の論者のなかには、私が『創価学会と平和主義』を公開情報のみによって書いたことを批判する向きもあった。「タテマエ的な公開情報だけ見ていては、創価学会の本質はわからない」という主旨の批判であった。

だが、私はそうは思わない。創価学会に限らず、巨大組織になればなるほど、「公開情報のなかでウソをつくこと」は難しくなっていくものである。組織防衛上の観点から表に出さない情報は当然あるとしても、虚偽の情報を出すことはリスクが大きすぎるし、組織が大きいほど矛盾も発覚しやすいからだ。

したがって、「公開情報だけを見ていても創価学会の本質は理解できない」というのは、短絡にすぎる見方だと思う。公開情報だけで十分な基本分析ができる。

では逆に、昔の週刊誌の創価学会批判記事のように、いわくつきの脱会者

（元学会員）や匿名の「事情通」からのリーク情報を集めたら、「創価学会の本質」とやらが理解できるのだろうか？　むしろ、歪んだプリズムによって本質が見えなくなってしまうだろう。

だから、公明党や創価学会を批判するにしても、怪しげな裏情報によるのではなく、公開情報を論拠とすべきなのだ。それは、まっとうな批判をするための大前提だろう。

「対中国」だけではない公明党外交の力

『五十年史』のなかで外交について論じた章として、第7章「日中国交回復実現へレール敷く」がある。一九七二年、当時の田中角栄内閣によって実現した日中国交正常化に、公明党が果たした大きな役割をまとめた内容である。

この章の最後に、『毎日新聞』論説委員・松田喬和氏の次のような言葉が引用されている。

「日中国交正常化は『公明党外交』の成果だった。外交交渉は政府の専権事項だと言われてきた。だが、日中国交正常化では野党であるにもかかわらず、公明党が果たした役割は大きかった」（第一法規『現代日本政党史録』第六巻）

この言葉が示すとおり、一般に「公明党と外交」と聞いてまず頭に浮かぶのは、対中外交への貢献であろう。特に日中国交正常化への道筋において、公明党が日本政府と中国の橋渡し役を果たしたことは、党史に輝く大きな成果と言える。

公明党が一九七〇年代から現在に至るまで保ち続けてきた、中国との太いつながり——それが日中関係の強化・改善にどれほど力となってきたかは、あらためて言うまでもない。

94

近年の例を挙げよう。

二〇一二年九月、当時の野田佳彦内閣は、中国の共産党大会（同年十一月）の直前という最悪のタイミングで尖閣諸島を国有化し、日中関係を大きく悪化させた。

だが、同年十二月の総選挙で自公連立政権が復活すると、その翌月には早くも、公明党の山口那津男代表が日中関係改善のために動いた。安倍晋三首相の親書を携え、訪中したのだ。そして、国家主席就任直前であった習近平氏と北京で会談し、「公明党は長期に中日友好に重要な役割を果たしてきた。政党間の交流をこれからも続けていきたい」「安倍首相にくれぐれもよろしくお伝えください。新たな中日関係への大きな貢献を期待している」との発言を引き出した。

また、山口代表は習近平氏との会談の席上、「次はわが党の若手議員との

交流を、ぜひやりましょう」と述べ、一三年秋には公明党の若手国会議員たちが訪中している。さらに、翌一四年六月には公明党の太田昭宏国土交通相(当時)も訪中し、中国の副首相と会談した。第二次安倍内閣発足以来、日本の閣僚が中国の副首相級と会談したのは、これが初めてであった。

要するに、袋小路に陥っていた中国との関係を、安倍政権発足後すぐに改善に向かわせたのは、公明党だったのだ。このこと一つとっても、日本の対

中国共産党の習近平総書記(当時・右)と会談する山口代表（2013 年 1 月 25 日、北京）

中外交に公明党が果たしてきた役割の大きさがわかる。

そのうえで指摘したいのは、「公明党が重要な役割を果たしてきたのは対中外交だけではない」ということだ。中国との強固な関係ばかりを強調してしまうと、公明党外交の幅広さが見えにくくなってしまう。ロシアや韓国、中東各国、米国などとの関係においても、公明党はそれぞれ重要な役割を果たしてきたのである。

先日刊行された、私と山口公明党代表との対談集『いま、公明党が考えていること』のなかで、私は次のように述べた。

「ソ連共産党が一番尊敬していたのは公明党です。『日本の政党の中で我々が一番大事にしなければいけないのは公明党だ』とソ連共産党の国際部の幹部がはっきり言っていました。(中略)一九八八年から九五年まで旧ソ連とロシアで外交官をやっていた私から見ると、ソ連・ロシアと日本の外交に公明党が及

97　第5章　外交でも重要な役割を果たしてきた公明党

ぼした役割は極めて大きいのです」

また、対米外交においては、公明党が政権にいることが日米関係の深化・重層化に結びついている。日米安保などにおいて、自民党のタカ派議員ばかりが主導してしまうと、対米関係のありようが偏(かたよ)ってしまう。公明党がバランサー(釣り合い装置)の役割を果たしているのだ。

公明党がバランサーとなった例として、二〇〇三年のイラク戦争への対応を挙げたい。イラク戦争は、当時のブッシュ(息子)米大統領が、イラクは大量破壊兵器を保有する「テロ国家」であるとして、英国などと共に武力行使に踏み切ったものであった。

公明党は自公政権内で、米英軍の武力行使に反対の姿勢を貫いた。たとえば、イラクへの攻撃が始まる直前の〇三年三月三日に、公明党は党訪米団を派遣。神崎武法(かんざきたけのり)代表(当時)は四日に米国務省でアーミテージ国務副長官(当時)

と会談し、最後まで平和的解決へ向けて努力することを強く要請した（一連の経緯は、『五十年史』の第17章「連立政権内で"歯止め役"も」に詳述）。ぎりぎりまで、平和を守るための対米外交に力を注いだのだ。

周知のとおり、米国がイラク攻撃の大義名分とした大量破壊兵器疑惑は、後に誤りであることがわかった。また、米国が開戦理由の一つに挙げていたフセイン大統領とテロ組織「アルカイダ」との関係もないことが判明した。このため、イラク戦争は「大義なき戦争」として世界中から批判を浴びた。そのことを考えれば、米国の対応を支持した小泉（純一郎）政権のなかにあって、公明党が武力行使反対の姿勢を貫いた（ただし、米国の対応を支持することについて、神崎代表は『苦渋の選択』と理解し、日本政府の立場としては、やむを得ない」とした）ことの意義は大きい。

池田会長の民間外交との連動

公明党の対中外交への大きな貢献は、創価学会の池田会長が中国と長年結んできた友好を土台としている。そもそも、中国側が国交正常化のパイプ役として公明党を"選んだ"のも、一九六〇年代から日中国交正常化を訴えていた池田会長への信頼ゆえである。

ことは対中関係に限らない。ロシアや韓国との関係など、公明党の外交はすべて、党の創立者である池田会長の民間外交が土台になっていると言ってよい。つまり、公明党外交は、池田会長の民間外交との"連動関係"を抜きにしては論じられないのだ。

私はかつて、「日本外交が池田会長に助けられているのはれっきとした事実

である」と書いたことがある(『潮』二〇〇七年十一月号「池田SGI会長の『民間外交』が果たす意義」)。

その記事のなかで例として挙げたのは、小泉政権下で悪化した対中関係を、第一次安倍政権が正常化させるに当たり、池田会長の持つチャンネルを見事に生かしたことであった。

また、池田会長の民間外交を各国が重視している証左として、中国の温家宝総理(当時)が二〇〇七年四月に来日した際、民間人としては唯一池田会長と会見したことなどを例に挙げた。

過去を振り返れば、特に見事な民間外交として、米ソ関係、中ソ関係が悪化した一九七四年から七五年にかけ、池田会長が米・中・ソ三国を相次いで訪れ、周恩来総理、ソ連のコスイギン首相、米国のキッシンジャー国務長官と会談し、関係改善の「橋渡し」をしたことが挙げられる。コスイギン首相との会見

において、「ソ連は中国を攻撃することも、孤立させる意図もない」との重要発言を引き出し、その後の中国訪問で周恩来総理に伝えたのである。これは、国家外交が行き詰まったときに民間外交が突破口を開いた稀有な例として、歴史に残るだろう。

元外交官である私の目から見ても、池田氏の外交センスは卓越している。

それはなぜかと考えるに、創価学会が世界宗教となっていくことを、池田氏が会長就任前から確信していたからこそだろう。

世界宗教になるためには、当然、世界各国との円滑な関係を築いていかなければならない。ゆえに、教団のトップリーダーには必然的に外交力が求められる。外交なくして世界宗教たり得ないのだ。創価学会を率いる責任感と、〝学会を世界宗教にさせずにおくものか〟という情熱が、池田氏の外交センスを育(はぐく)んだのだと思う。

池田会長は、民間外交の持つ意義について、次のように述べている。

「外交官を中心とした外交関係はもちろん大切です。と同時に、そうした〝国家の代表〟の立場とは別に、国益という枠を超える次元での交流が必要になってきています。（中略）従来の国家外交は国益という枠内でしか、ものが見えない硬直性をもっていました。それに対し、民間外交は『国家の顔』でなく、『人間の顔』を表にたてることができるという利点をもちます」（ノーマン・カズンズとの対談集『世界市民の対話』〈聖教文庫〉）

そのような池田会長の広範な民間外交を土台とし、さらに世界百九十二カ国・地域に広がるSGIのネットワークとも連動しているからこそ、公明党外交は大きな力を発揮できる。それは、国家外交でありながら、民衆の視点に立った外交でもあるからだ。

つけ加えれば、「池田会長の民間外交が公明党外交の土台になっている」と

は、池田氏が公明党に対して指示をしているという意味ではない。池田会長が平和に向けて努力し、対話し、行動してきた姿そのものが、公明党の議員に強い精神的影響を与えているという意味である。

東アジアの平和に対する大きな貢献

これは公明党外交の事例ではないのだが、重要な出来事なので触れておきたい。

二〇一六年三月十日付の『聖教新聞』の一つの記事に、私は強い印象を受けた。創価学会の原田稔(みのる)会長が訪韓し、韓国・慶南(キョンナム)大学の朴在圭(パクチェギュ)総長と会見を行ったという記事である。記事としてはそれほどの分量ではなかったから、気づかなかった『聖教新聞』読者の皆さんもいたかもしれない。しかし、これは

大きな意義を持つ会見である。

周知のとおり、一六年に入ってから朝鮮半島の緊張が非常に高まっている。北朝鮮は一月六日に地下核実験（自称「水爆実験」）を強行し、二月にはまたも弾道ミサイルを発射。そうした動きに呼応して、韓国では「核武装論」までが主張され始めた。たとえば、韓国の最大紙『朝鮮日報』は、一月二十八日付の社説で「米中に頼れない韓国、今こそ独自の核武装を」と論じるなど、「核武装やむなし」との論陣を堂々と張るようになった。東アジアに〝熱核戦争〟が勃発する危険は、かなり現実味を帯びてきている。

原田会長による三月の訪韓は、そうした危機的状況をふまえ、「日本最大の宗教団体の長として、今こそやらねばならない焦眉の課題は何か？」を思索したうえでの行動に違いない。すなわち、東アジアの平和を守るための行動だったのだ。

慶南大学の朴総長との会見が行われた場所は、北韓大学院大学。北朝鮮との和解に向けて努力している大学で、朴総長は同大の創立者でもある。しかも、会見では〝慶南大学と創価大学が力を合わせ、平和研究の人材を育てていきましょう〟との話がなされたという。

この会見の意図は明らかだ。朝鮮半島の緊張が高まっている現状のなかで、核戦争の危機を取り除くために力を合わせようというアピールだったのである。

原田会長は宗教者であるから、政治の領域には直接踏み込まず、大学に行った。それも、朝鮮半島での有事を回避するためにふさわしい大学と相手を選んで、会見を行った。そして、池田会長が創立した創価大学との連携を強めることによって、日韓の平和勢力の強化を図ったのだ。

北韓大学院大学は二〇一五年五月、池田会長に「名誉碩座教授」の称号を授与している。原田会長が同大学を訪問するまでに、十分な関係が築かれていた

のである。

　また、韓国にはすでに百五十万人を超えるSGIメンバーがいる。これは韓国の人口(約五千二百万人)のおよそ三十五分の一に当たる数で、韓国人の三十五人に一人以上がSGIメンバーなのである。

　そのように、韓国との間に重層的な関係をつくり、韓国内でもSGIが大きな勢力になっているからこそ、原田会長の訪韓と対話は東アジアの平和のための具体的な力になるのだ。

　原田会長の訪韓は、池田会長の平和思想を見事に体現した行動であった。また、創価大学に創立者の平和思想がきちんと根付いていることを示す出来事でもあった。東アジアの平和にとって、また、創価学会の悲願である「核廃絶」という大目標にとって、すこぶる重要な意義があったと思う。

　そしてもちろん、公明党も今後、こうした行動を政治外交の面から支える動

きをしていくはずだ。
　そのように、SGIと公明党はそれぞれの領域から、池田会長の平和思想を体現する役割を果たしている。その相乗効果が、東アジア、ひいては世界の平和に果たす役割は、極めて大きい。

第6章

公明党「与党化」の意義を考える

「与党化」への軌跡を刻みつけた党史

『五十年史』の前半は、公明党の野党時代の歴史が綴られているが、第12章「歴史的な細川連立政権に参加」からは、与党になってからの話が中心になる。

「与党としての公明党」は、一九九三年の細川（護熙）連立政権参加によって始まり、九九年からの自民党との連立政権（当初は「自由党」も参加の自自公連立）時代に本格化した。

しかし、その前の野党時代にも、現在のような与党化に向けての地ならしともいうべき局面が、何度もあった。たとえば、七二年の日中国交正常化に際して、野党であった公明党が中国と田中角栄内閣の橋渡しをしたことは、その一つと言える。

また、短命に終わった新進党への参加（九四～九七年）も、「与党になるためのトレーニングだった」と考えれば、公明党にとって重要な意義を持っていたと言えよう。

さらに、『五十年史』の第11章「PKO法成立を主導」は、次のような印象的な一節で結ばれている。

「公明党にとって、（湾岸戦争での）90億ドル支援問題からPKO法成立までの経験は、当時野党でありながら国の新しい生き方の決定に関（かか）わり、党自体も議員も鍛えられ与党的な経験を積んだ。結果として、政権与党へのトレーニングになり、後の細川政権の実現、自民党との連立政権参加につながった」

そのように、結党以来の約三十年間にわたる野党時代であっても、公明党は与党になることを目指して着実な前進を続けてきたのである。『五十年史』は、"与党化"への軌跡を刻みつけた党史"とも言える。

今回は、公明党が「与党化」したことの意義について、掘り下げて考えてみよう。

世界宗教の「与党化」は必然である

一宗教者・一神学徒である私の目から見れば、公明党の与党化は必然であり、何ら不思議なことでも意外なことでもない。

なぜなら、公明党の支持母体・創価学会は、SGIとしての世界宗教化のただ中にあるからだ。歴史を振り返っても、「世界宗教と結びついた政党は与党であるのが当たり前」であり、野党であるほうがむしろ不自然なのだ。

たとえばキリスト教は、西暦三一三年の「ミラノ勅令」によってローマ帝国の公認宗教となり、「与党化」した。現代においても、ドイツでメルケル首相

の所属する「キリスト教民主同盟」(CDU)が長年与党であるなど、「世界宗教の与党化」の例は枚挙に暇がない。

つまり、創価学会の本格的な世界宗教化と公明党の与党化は、コインの両面のように密接にリンクしているのだ。

ではなぜ、世界宗教の「与党化」は必然なのだろうか。

一つには、世界宗教というものが、「反体制的ではなく、既存の社会システムを認めたうえで"体制内改革"を進めていく」という共通の特徴を持っているからである。

創価学会もしかり。「人間革命」というキーワードが誤解を招きがちだが、創価学会に革命によって既存の国家権力を打倒するという発想はまったくない。「人間革命」は体制転覆の革命ではなく"人々の心のなかからの革命"を指すのであり、創価学会はあくまで現実的改革を目指す教団なのである。

各国のSGI組織のありようを見ても、その国の基礎的な政治の原則に触れるような行為は決して行わず、既存の社会システムにすんなり溶け込んでいる。

そして、世界宗教が体制内改革を標榜（ひょうぼう）するものである以上、その改革を進めるためにいちばん力を持った存在である与党と結びつくのは必然なのだ。現実への影響力という点で、野党と与党には天地の差がある。与党になってこそ、日本一国を大きく動かす力を得ることができるのだ。そのことは、野党時代の公明党と与党となってからの公明党を比べるだけでも一目瞭然（いちもくりょうぜん）だろう。

与党だからこそ持ち得た「影響力」の例

ここでは、公明党が与党だからこそ持ち得た影響力の例として、三つのこと

を挙げたい。

第一に、平和安全法制成立までの経緯において、公明党が果たした「歯止め」の役割である。

私は、二〇一四年七月の「国の存立を全(まっと)うし、国民を守るための切れ目のない安全保障法制の整備について」の閣議決定の時点から、「公明党が歯止めをかけ、戦争につながるような動きを封印した」と評価してきた。一方、閣議決定の時点から「公明党はこれで『平和の党』の看板を下ろした」と批判し、平和安全法制についても「戦争法」と呼んで批判を続ける勢力がある。

では、閣議決定から約二年を経た今、現実はどうなっているだろうか。

南シナ海の南沙(なんさ)諸島では中国が人工島を建設し、米国がその軍事拠点化を危惧(ぐ)して「航行の自由」作戦と称するイージス艦派遣を行った。米中の軍事衝突が起こりかねない緊迫した状態が、今も続いている。しかし、「日本も同盟

国たる米国を守るため、南沙諸島に自衛隊を派遣すべきだ」などという話は、まったく出ていない。もしも平和安全法制がなければ、日本はNSC（国家安全保障会議）による判断で、自衛隊のP‐3C哨戒機くらい飛ばしていたことは十分考えられる。それがなかったこと自体、平和安全法制が歯止めになっていることの明白な証左である。

同様に、シリアなどで起きているIS（「イスラム国」）をめぐる一連の危機のなかで、「米軍が中東に行くならば、自衛隊も応分の貢献をすべきだ」という議論は、すでに出ていた。しかし、現実には中東への自衛隊派遣はまったくなされていない。これも、公明党が平和安全法制にかけた歯止め——具体的には、閣議決定に盛り込まれた「武力行使の新3要件」——のたまものである。

そして、そのように歯止めがかけられる力を持ち得たのも、公明党が自民党と連立与党を組んでいるからこそなのだ。

仮に公明党が平和安全法制に反対して政権を離脱していたとしても、そのことが現実の平和につながったとは思えない。自民党が他党の右派勢力と手を組んで、歯止めのない平和安全法制となり、今ごろは南沙諸島や中東に自衛隊が派遣されていたかもしれない。政府のなかには自衛隊を地球の反対側まで送りたい人たちがいる。しかし、実際には自衛隊の派遣がそう容易ではないことが、一連の議論を通じてはっきりした。だから軽々には派遣できなくなってきた。あえて言えば、公明党は単に「歯止め」をかけたにとどまらず、自衛隊をめぐる「構造」そのものを変化させたのだ。

二つ目の例は、二〇一五年八月十四日に発表された、安倍晋三首相の「戦後七十年談話」である。

あの談話は、当初マスコミが予想していたものよりもはるかにバランスの取れた内容になった。最大のポイントは、「満州事変、そして国際連盟からの脱

退。日本は、次第に、国際社会が壮絶な犠牲の上に築こうとした『新しい国際秩序』への『挑戦者』となっていった。進むべき針路を誤り、戦争への道を進んで行きました」という一節である。

「満州事変以後の日本の歩みは誤っていた」との歴史認識は、創価学会や池田SGI会長の歴史認識に近い。満州事変以後、日本は池田会長の言う「国家主義という誤った宗教」にとらわれ、会長が「戦争ほど、残酷なものはない。戦争ほど、悲惨なものはない」と『人間革命』の冒頭に記した、その戦争への道を突き進んでいったからだ。

一九九五年、戦後五十年の節目に当たって発表された、当時の村山（富市）首相の談話は、日本の植民地支配と侵略で各国が被った「損害と苦痛」に謝罪を表明するものではあったが、「遠くない過去の一時期、国策を誤り」と表現するにとどまっていた。

「遠くない過去の一時期」の誤りとは、日米開戦とも考えられるし、「ポツダム宣言」受諾を当初拒否して原爆投下を招いたこととも考えられる。どうとでも解釈可能なように、あえてぼかしたのだろう。だが、時期を明確にしなければ、歴史認識の表明としても、謝罪表明としても、ほとんど意味をなさないのである。

つまり、日本が道を誤った時期を明確に特定した点で、社会党委員長であった村山の談話より、むしろ安倍首相の談話のほうが踏み込んだ内容になっていたのだ。これは、安倍首相が連立パートナーの公明党に配慮したからにほかならない。安倍首相は、発表直後を除けば、戦後七十年談話についてほとんど言及していないが、それは、あの談話が彼にとって必ずしも本意ではないことを示していると思う。公明党が与党であることによって持ち得た影響力の、実例の一つと言える。

三つ目の例は、軽減税率導入決定までの経緯である。結果的には、公明党の主張をほぼ丸のみする形で、自民党も軽減税率導入に同意した。これも、公明党が与党であるからこそだろう。

そのように、ここ一、二年の動向に限っても、安全保障・歴史認識・財政という三つの分野において、公明党が自民党に大きな影響力を及ぼしてきたのだ。国会議員の数から言えば自民党の約八分の一しかいない公明党が、今や日本の舵取りをしていると言っても過言ではない。

つけ加えるなら、オバマ米大統領の広島訪問決定も、間接的には「公明党が与党にいるからこそ実現した」ものだと、私は考えている。

一九五七年に当時の戸田城聖第二代会長がいち早く「原水爆禁止宣言」を発した創価学会は、「核兵器――現代世界の脅威展」をニューヨークの国連本部を皮切りに各国で巡回展示するなど、核廃絶への世論を喚起してきた。そのよ

うな創価学会が支持母体となった公明党が政権にいることの意味を、オバマ政権は重々承知しているはずである。

核なき世界についての理念や取り組みを理由にノーベル平和賞を受賞したオバマ大統領だからこそ、核廃絶を悲願として掲げる創価学会の平和運動に、シンパシー（共感）も感じているに違いない。

「与党化」とは、現実の政治においてそれほどの力を持つということなのである。特にここ一、二年は、自民党と

結党50年を迎えた公明党の全国大会（2014年9月21日）

の長い連立期間の蓄積もあって、公明党の影響力はますます大きくなっている。野党時代から長く公明党を支持してきた学会員ほど、与党化によって公明党が得た力の大きさをしみじみと実感されているのではないだろうか。

「成長戦略」でもある公明党の福祉政策

公明党は今後も与党であり続けると思うが、そのことは日本にとってどのような意味を持つだろうか。

まず、日本の平和、アジアの平和にとって、公明党は重要な役割を果たしていくに違いない。この点は、第五章の論考などで詳述したとおりである。

そして私は、経済政策においても、公明党が日本を大きく変えていくと考えている。なぜなら、自民党とは経済に取り組む姿勢自体が大きく異なるからで

ある。

自民党は昔も今も大企業の代弁者としてのカラーが強く、その経済政策は「トリクルダウン」を基本としている。つまり、"大企業や富裕層が今よりも潤えば、そのおこぼれがやがて中小企業・庶民の側にもトリクルダウン（＝したたり落ちる）する"という発想が、根底にあるのだ。

それに対して、「大衆とともに語り、大衆とともに戦い、大衆の中に死んでいく」を永遠の立党精神として掲げる公明党は、経済政策においても常に大衆を中心に考えている。"大衆の生活がより豊かになってこそ、日本全体が豊かになる"というのが基本的な考え方であり、いわば「ボトムアップ型」の経済政策が、公明党流なのである。

近年、「トリクルダウン理論」は実証的に否定されつつある。OECD（経済協力開発機構）の実証研究などにより、富裕層や大企業だけが潤っても、そ

の「おこぼれ」で中小企業や大衆が豊かになることはなく、むしろ格差拡大が経済成長を抑制する、と見られるようになってきたのだ。それは言い換えれば、「レーガノミクス」(一九八〇年代にロナルド・レーガン米大統領が取った経済政策)以来の自由主義・新自由主義的経済政策が、理論的にも現実的にも破綻したということでもある。

そうした世界的趨勢を見るに、公明党が与党であることは、経済政策面でも大きな意義を持っていると感じる。「政治の谷間」に放置されていた庶民に光を当てるべく誕生した公明党は、昔も今も庶民層の生活改善を最重視してきた。その政治姿勢が、実は日本経済全体の活性化にもつながるということが、ようやくはっきりしてきたからである。

かつて、福祉政策は「枯れ木に水」とか「バラマキ」などと呼ばれ、軽んじられていた。その時代から公明党は一貫して福祉を重視し、貧困層にも平等に

教育の機会を与えることに力を注いできた。義務教育における教科書無償配布は草創期の公明党の輝かしい実績であるし、奨学金の拡充（成績要件の撤廃など）にも努めてきた。

バブル経済崩壊以来の「失われた二十年」を経て、今や子どもの六人に一人が貧困状態に置かれているのが日本である。だからこそ、これからの日本では貧困対策こそが喫緊の課題であり、それは公明党が与党にいてこそ成し遂げられることだ。自民党だけでは、実りある貧困対策はできないと思う。なぜなら、自民党は富裕層重視の姿勢が骨がらみになっており、彼らが考える貧困対策は、どうしても〝おこぼれを分け与える〟かのような「上から目線」のものになりがちだからである。

しかし、大衆とともに進んできた公明党は、庶民の心の機微がよくわかっている。だからこそ、公明党の福祉政策は、公助・共助・自助のバランスが取れ

ている。国からの保護が必要な人には保護を与え、自立を促すべき人には背中を押して促すという、ケース・バイ・ケースの対応ができるのだ。

そして、貧困対策は単なる「バラマキ」ではなく、長期的視野で考えれば最大の「成長戦略」でもある。そのことは、貧困問題の専門家も、つとに指摘していることである。

たとえば阿部彩氏（首都大学東京教授）は、著書『子どもの貧困Ⅱ──解決策を考える』（岩波新書）のなかで、次のように述べている。

「子どもの貧困に対する政策は、短期的には社会への見返りはないかもしれない。しかし、長期的にみれば、これらの政策は、その恩恵を受けた子どもの所得が上がり、税金や社会保険料を支払い、GDPに貢献するようになるので、ペイするのである。すなわち、子どもの貧困対策は『投資』なのである。子どもが成人するまでに、長くは二〇年かかるので、この『投資』は長期的な観

点で見なければならない。しかし、『費用』ではなく『投資』と考えることによって、政策の優先順位も変わってくるであろう。たとえば、貧困の子どもに、ただ単に最低限の『衣食住』だけを提供するプログラムと、その子どもに『衣食住プラス教育』を提供するプログラムがあった場合、たとえ後者のほうが費用が高いとしても、投資のリターンとしては前者よりも後者のほうが優れているのは自明である」

「トリクルダウン理論」が破綻した今、"成長戦略としての貧困対策"に、日本は取り組んでいくべきである。それはすぐには成果が出なかったとしても、十年、二十年という長いスパンで見た場合、「良き納税者をつくる」ことによって、日本経済を上向かせるのである。逆に、貧困対策から目をそらしていたなら、いわゆる「貧困の連鎖」が断ち切れず、貧困層の子どもはまた貧困層になってしまう。そして、納税できず、社会的扶助によって生活する層が拡大

127　第6章　公明党「与党化」の意義を考える

すればするほど、必然的に日本経済も停滞するのである。

公明党が過去五十年間やってきた政策には、常に「未来の良き納税者をつくる」という観点があり、"成長戦略としての貧困対策"に相当するものが多かった。公明党が政権のなかにいて、金持ち寄りになりがちな自民党の政策を軌道修正している意義は大きい。

すべての人々を守る「人間主義」を掲げて

本書のためにあらためて『五十年史』を熟読してみて、私がしみじみと感じたのは、「公明党は結党以来、その姿勢にまったくブレがない」ということである。

と言うと、首をかしげる人もあるかもしれない。公明党は、批判者から「コ

ウモリ政党」と揶揄されることも少なくないからだ。敵対した時期もある自民党と連立を組んでいることなど、表面的な出来事だけを見れば、そう見えてしまう面もあるだろう。

だが、そうではない。公明党は常に「大衆にとっての最善」を考えて行動してきたのであり、その一点においてまったくブレがないのだ。

公明党は、「国民」よりも「大衆」という言葉に重きを置いてきた。なぜ「国民」ではなく「大衆」なのかといえば、「国民」は「日本国籍を有する者」という意味になり、「日本国籍を持たずに日本に住んでいる人」——在日外国人や無国籍者を排除するニュアンスを孕むからだろう。

もちろん、政治のある局面においては、日本国籍を持つ人だけを対象とせざるを得ないこともある。それでも基本的には、政治の主体は「その国に住むすべての人」なのである。

同様に、「生活者」という言葉を最初に前面に出した政党も、公明党だ。

国民ではなく、「大衆」「生活者」――公明党の用いるワーディング（言い回し）には、国籍にかかわらず、そこに住むすべての人々を守っていこうとする姿勢が感じられる。

一部の人ではなく、すべての人のための政治。日本一国のみならず、世界のための政治。そのような「人間主義」、世界市民的な視野を持った政治を、公明党は半世紀余にわたって貫いてきたのだ。

The party often uses the term "masses" rather than "citizens." The reason is that the word "citizen" implies a person who holds Japanese nationality; it suggests the exclusion of other residents in Japan who do not hold citizenship, such as foreigners or stateless persons.

Of course, some aspects of politics only apply to Japanese nationals, but in essence the main constituents of politics should be all residents of that nation.

Komeito was the political party that first brought the term *seikatsusha*, which can be loosely translated as "people leading ordinary lives," into public discourse.

Their use of terms such as *taishu*—the masses—and seikatsusha rather than "citizens," represents their attitude to protect all people in the country regardless of their nationality: politics not just for a portion of people or for merely a single nation, but for all people and the entire world. This is the humanistic approach to politics—the politics of global citizenship—that Komeito has pursued for the past half century.

are not implemented, children currently in poverty will become impoverished adults, trapping Japan in a cycle of poverty. Without a sufficient tax base, an increasing number of people dependent on government benefits will only result in increasing stagnation in the economy.

Komeito's polices over the past fifty years have been grounded in this perspective of expanding tax revenue base; many of its policies could be considered poverty alleviation growth strategies. The party's presence in government is thus significant from this perspective too—correcting the LDP's tendencies to create policy that favors the wealthy.

A universal humanism

Rereading the *Chronicle*, what truly impresses me is that since its establishment, Komeito's political stance has remained resolute.

Some may question this statement, given that Komeito has been criticized for shifting to whichever way the political winds may blow. At face value, Komeito forming a coalition with the LDP, with whom the party was once at odds, may seem to bear this out.

Not so, however. Komeito's advance has always been about what is best for the masses. This is a stance from which it has never wavered.

national development. Experts on poverty issues have always known this.

Professor Aya Abe of Tokyo Metropolitan University, for example, states in her book "Child Poverty II: Rethinking Solution Strategy" (Iwanami Shoten, 2014) that while child poverty policies may yield low returns for society in the short-term, in the long run people who benefitted from these policies as children will have greater incomes, generating more tax revenues and social insurance premiums. This will contribute to the GDP. Such policies, therefore, do pay. In other words, child poverty policies are an investment. Since it may take up to twenty years for children to come of age, it is a long-term investment. However, when such policies are recognized as an investment rather than an expense, the order of priorities will change. For instance, if one program merely offers a destitute child the minimum basic needs of food, clothing and shelter, and another offers food, clothing, shelter, plus education, even if the latter costs more, it is quite obvious which will yield a higher return on investment.

With trickle-down theory having failed, it would be wise for Japan to consider implementing poverty alleviation measures as a national growth strategy. Results would not be immediate, but in ten or twenty years, the growth in the tax revenue base is likely to ensue in an upturn in the Japanese economy. On the other hand, if poverty alleviation measures compulsory education students in its early years is a shining achievement, and the party has also been instrumental in improving the national scholarship system (by eliminating eligibility based on grades).

Following the "Lost Score" or "Lost Twenty Years" since the collapse of the bubble economy in Japan, one in six children is now considered to be living in poverty. Measures to fight poverty will therefore be of utmost importance to the future of Japan, and the implementation of such measures is assured with Komeito in government. The LDP alone will not be able to deliver on this. The mentality of siding with the wealthy is so deeply rooted in the LDP that when it comes to tackling poverty, Liberal Democrats are unable to get over their tendency of looking down on people—"granting them a share" from the tricklings of their wealth.

Komeito, however, has always been among the masses and understands the people. Because of this, the party's welfare policies strike a balance between mutual assistance, public assistance and self-help. As such, the aim is to provide assistance on a case-by-case basis, with the government offering needy individuals with direct support while those who can be encouraged to become self-reliant benefit from programs to meet their needs.

Besides, anti-poverty measures are not handouts but, from a long-term perspective, represent the surest strategy for ordinary people are enriched.

In recent years, the trickle-down theory has been empirically refuted. Studies conducted by the Organization for Economic Cooperation and Development (OECD) have shown that the benefits accrued solely from the earnings of the wealthy and large businesses do not extend to smaller businesses. Rather, the widening disparity inhibits economic growth. In other words, since the Reaganomics policies promoted by US President Ronald Reagan during the 1980s, free-market and neoliberal policies of the past and present have failed, both in theory and in practice.

In the face of such global trends, Komeito's position as a governing party has great significance with regard to economic policy. Komeito, which emerged to bring attention to ordinary people who were essentially marginalized in politics, has always assigned top priority to improving the livelihood of the masses. It is finally becoming apparent that this political approach is in fact linked to the revitalization of Japanese economy.

In the past, social welfare policies have been mocked as an exercise in futility ("watering a dead tree") or as lavish handouts. From the outset, Komeito has emphasized the importance of social welfare and made efforts to provide equal educational opportunities to the poor and underprivileged. Its provision of free textbooks for leverage over the LDP. More than anyone, it is the Soka Gakkai members who have supported Komeito since its time as an opposition party, who truly appreciate the influence Komeito has obtained by being a governing party.

Social welfare as a national growth strategy

Komeito will most likely remain a partner in the present coalition government, but what will this mean for Japan? First of all, Komeito will play an important role for peace in Japan and Asia, as I have already discussed in Chapter 5. It will also significantly change Japan in areas of economic policy, owing to the fact that their approach to economic issues is vastly different from that of the LDP.

The LDP has traditionally been and remains tainted by their stance as a mouthpiece for large corporations espousing "trickle-down economics"—the idea that if large businesses or the wealthy prosper, the effect will eventually benefit small- and medium-sized enterprises as well as the public.

Contrary to this idea, Komeito upholds a founding principle of serving the people to the very end through dialogue and political struggle and has always operated on the basis of what is best for the people, including in economic policy. The party's economic policy is a bottom-up model based on the core belief that Japan will prosper only when the lives of finance. In number, Komeito may only be one-eighth of the size of the LDP in parliament, but it would be no exaggeration to say that it is the Komeito that is steering Japan at this time.

Additionally, I believe US President Barak Obama's decision to visit Hiroshima was also indirectly as a consequence of Komeito being a member of Japan's coalition government.

Since as early as 1957, when second Soka Gakkai President Josei Toda made a declaration calling for the abolition of nuclear weapons, the Soka Gakkai has been involved in rallying public support for nuclear disarmament. It has done this, for example, by organizing exhibitions such as "Nuclear Arms: Threat to Our World," which was first shown at the UN Headquarters in New York and later toured the world. The Obama administration must surely know the significance of having Komeito, supported by an organization like the Soka Gakkai, in government.

As a Nobel Peace Prize laureate himself, awarded for his promotion of nuclear abolition, President Obama would likely sympathize with the Soka Gakkai's peace movement calling for the abolition of nuclear weapons.

This shows the extent to which the party's real-world political influence is increased by being in the ruling coalition. Considering its long partnership in the coalition, the past two years in particular have seen a notable increase in Komeito's response by Japan to the Potsdam Declaration, which culminated in the dropping of the atomic bomb. The statement was most likely left vague so it could be interpreted in any way. However, a statement acknowledging history or a statement of apology is pointless if it does not address a specific period in time.

In that sense, having clarified the time at which Japan took the wrong course, the statement by Abe has greater depth than that made by Murayama, who headed the Social Democratic Party. This is nothing less than Abe's consideration toward his coalition partner, Komeito. Apart from comments made immediately after the statement, Abe hasn't discussed the statement, and I believe this indicates that the contents of the statement aren't necessarily his own. This is another example of what Komeito has been able to accomplish through its influence as a ruling party.

The third example is the sequence of events that led to the decision to defer the proposed consumption tax increase on basic necessities for low-income earners. The LDP ultimately agreed to the deferment, acceding to almost all of Komeito's terms. This could only have happened with Komeito in the ruling coalition.

These events in the past two years alone demonstrate Komeito's considerable influence on the LDP in the three areas of national security, historical awareness and national

With the Manchurian Incident, followed by the withdrawal from the League of Nations, Japan gradually transformed itself into a challenger to the new international order that the international community sought to establish after tremendous sacrifices. Japan took the wrong course and advanced along the road to war.

The historical perspective that Japan's course of action after the Manchurian Incident was wrong is similar to that of Mr. Ikeda and the Soka Gakkai. Following the incident, Japan became ensnared with what Mr. Ikeda once described as the erroneous religion of nationalism. Its erroneousness is proved by Japan's advance along the path to war. As Mr. Ikeda noted in the opening lines of his novel, *The Human Revolution*, "Nothing is more barbarous than war. Nothing is more cruel."

The statement made by Prime Minister Tomiichi Murayama in 1995 on the fiftieth anniversary of the end of war expressed remorse for the "tremendous damage and suffering" inflicted on the people of many countries by Japan's colonial rule and aggression. However, it went no further than calling it a "mistaken national policy during a certain period in the not too distant past."

A mistake in "a certain period in the not too distant past" could refer to the start of the Pacific War or to the unofficial

Chapter 6　As a Party in Ruling Coalitions

the brakes applied by Komeito in the peace and national security legislation—specifically the "three new conditions of the use of military force" that were incorporated in the cabinet decision. Komeito had the power to apply these brakes because of its position as a coalition partner in government with the LDP.

Even supposing Komeito opposed the peace and security legislation and withdrew from the coalition government, the end result would not have been peace. The LDP may simply have joined hands with right-leaning parties to pass legislation that would not have the restrictions it does now, and would have dispatched SDF troops to the South China Sea and the Middle East by now. Some hardliners in government are determined to send the SDF to far corners of the world.

However, it has become clear through the debate over the legislation in the Diet that dispatching troops is not that easy in reality. The deployment of troops cannot be readily tasked. Komeito not only put the brakes on these procedures but in fact transformed the overall structure in which the SDF operates.

The second example I would like to cite is the statement made by Prime Minister Shinzo Abe on August 14, 2015, commemorating the seventieth anniversary of the end of war. This statement turned out to be more balanced than was expected by the media. The crux being this passage:

the Komeito has served to halt any moves that may lead to war. Meanwhile, the party has been accused of relinquishing its trademark pacifism. There has also been a continuous barrage of criticism of the 2015 legislation, calling it a "law for war."

What then is actually occurring now, some two years after this cabinet decision?

When China created an artificial island in the Spratly Islands in the South China Sea, the US, fearing it would be used as a military base, dispatched warships under the Freedom of Navigation Operation (FONOP). Even now, tension continues over a possible outbreak of military conflict between the US and China. However, in Japan, there is no mention of sending Japanese troops to the Spratly Islands to support the nation Japan is allied with. If not for the peace and security legislation, which requires deliberations by the Japanese National Security Council (NSC), it is highly probable that Japan would have at least deployed Self Defense Force P-3C patrol planes by now. The fact that they haven't is clear proof that the 2015 legislation has acted as a brake.

Similarly, with regard to the ISIS crisis in, for example, Syria, an argument had been raised that if US armed forces are being deployed in the Middle East, the SDF should also do its part. In reality, however, no SDF troops have been dispatched to the Middle East. This can be attributed again to demonstrated that the organization never behaves in a way that may infringe on the fundamental principles or character of the nation. SGI organizations easily blend with the existing social system.

As long as world religions espouse this kind of reformation from within, I feel it is inevitable that they unite with the most influential ruling party to advance such reform.

There is a world of difference between ruling parties and opposition parties with regard to their ability to accomplish such reformation. Only the ruling party truly has the authority to move the nation. And this difference is as plain as day when one compares Komeito in the opposition and Komeito as a ruling party.

Influence as a ruling party

I will cite three examples of the level of influence Komeito has been able to exert as a result of being in the current ruling coalition.

First is the role it played as a restraint on government in the events leading up to the enactment of the 2015 Japan peace and national security legislation.

As I have pointed out elsewhere, since the cabinet decision on the "Development of seamless security legislation to ensure Japan's survival and protect its people" in July 2014, parties and world religions. More accurately, it would be senseless for a world religion be linked to an opposition party.

For instance, the Edict of Milan in 313 AD gave Christianity legal status within the Roman Empire, virtually making it a governing party. Today, the CDU in Germany, headed by Chancellor Angela Merkel, is a ruling party and has been for many years. There are countless other examples of world religions being connected to a ruling party.

In other words, like two sides of a coin, the Soka Gakkai becoming a world religion is closely linked to the Komeito becoming a ruling party.

Why do I say that it is a foregone conclusion that world religions are associated with the ruling party?

One reason is that world religions have the common characteristic of promoting reform from within; they embrace conventional social principles and are not anti-establishment.

This applies to the Soka Gakkai as well. Its ideal of "human revolution" could easily be misinterpreted, but the Soka Gakkai lacks any notion of upending the existing national power structure through some revolution. Human revolution refers not to the overturning of the establishment but to the practical, everyday struggle to achieve an inner transformation. The Soka Gakkai, then, is most definitely an organization that strives for reformation from within the establishment.

Individual SGI organizations around the world have

Chapter 6 As a Party in Ruling Coalitions

For Komeito, being involved in the decision making on Japan's new course— from the issue of the $9 billion of support [for the Gulf War] to the enactment of the PKO [Peacekeeping Operations] law—while still in the opposition was good training. It enabled the party and its members to experience something akin to being a ruling party. This helped prepare us for when we came into power with the establishment of the Hosokawa administration, then later with the LDP-Komeito coalition.

Thus, while in the opposition, Komeito steadily paved the way to becoming a ruling party over some three decades from the time of its formation. The *Chronicle* could also be regarded as a history of this journey.

This chapter will explore the significance of Komeito taking office as a ruling party.

World religions and ruling parties

From my perspective as a religious person and a theologian, there is nothing surprising about Komeito becoming a member of a ruling coalition. I see it, in fact, as an inevitability.

My reason for saying so is that their supporting organization, the Soka Gakkai (as SGI), is in the midst of establishing itself as a world religion. History shows the link between ruling

Chapter 6

As a Party in Ruling Coalitions

The first half of the *Chronicle* outlines Komeito's history as an opposition party. However, from Chapter 12, the focus shifts to its history as a member of a ruling coalition. This history began in 1993 with the party's participation in the multi-party Morihiro Hosokawa coalition cabinet; in 1999 Komeito became a major player when it partnered with the Liberal Democratic Party in a coalition government that was initially also joined by the now defunct Liberal Party.

It is apparent, however, that the groundwork for becoming a ruling party was laid while it was still in the opposition. One instance of this is its acting as an intermediary between China and the Kakuei Tanaka cabinet to help normalize Sino-Japanese relations in 1972, which it did as an opposition party.

Even its short-lived participation in the New Frontier Party (1994-1997) could be considered training for becoming a ruling party.

Chapter 11 of the *Chronicle* concludes with the following:

As this shows, both the SGI and Komeito function in their respective domains to put Mr. Ikeda's peace ideals into practice. The role this synergy plays in peace building in not just East Asia but the entire world is immense.

his boundaries into politics, he visited a university. Not just any university, mind you; he chose a university most suitable for circumventing emergency situations on the Korean Peninsula. And by strengthening ties between Kyungnam University and the university that Mr. Ikeda founded, Mr. Harada was attempting to simultaneously strengthen ties between Japan and South Korea for the sake of peace.

In May 2015, the University of North Korean Studies awarded Mr. Ikeda with the title of Honorary Chair Professor. The connection was already established prior to Mr. Harada's visit to the university.

In addition, the SGI membership in South Korea reaches over 1.5 million, meaning that one in 35 people in South Korea is an SGI member.

Owing to these multilayered relations and the growing presence of SGI members in South Korea, I believe Mr. Harada's visit to and dialogue in that country will lead to real momentum for peace in East Asia.

The visit was an endeavor that squarely embodied Mr. Ikeda's ideals for peace. It also confirmed that the founder's peace ideals are firmly rooted in Soka University. For peace in East Asia, and for the Soka Gakkai's worthy goal of nuclear weapons abolition, this visit was genuinely meaningful.

Komeito will naturally take action in the future to enhance such moves from the standpoint of political diplomacy.

Chapter 5   A Key Agent in Diplomacy

to growing calls for nuclear armament in South Korea. For example, the editorial of the January 28 edition of *The Chosun Ilbo*, a major South Korean newspaper, argued that South Korea could no longer depend on the US or China and that the time had come to deploy its own nuclear weapons. It boldly made the case that nuclear armament is inevitable. The risk of a nuclear war breaking out in East Asia suddenly began to seem all too real.

I am certain Mr. Harada's visit to South Korea in March was a result of deliberating the best course of action to take as a leader of Japan's largest religious organization in the midst of this crisis. Therefore, it was action taken to help protect the peace in East Asia.

The meeting with the Kyungnam University president took place on the campus of the University of North Korean Studies. This institution is known for its North Korean studies and proposals to settle issues between Noth and South Korea peacefully, and President Park is its founder. During the meeting, they discussed Kyungnam University and Soka University working together to foster capable people through peace studies.

The significance of this meeting is quite clear. In the midst of rising tensions on the Korean Peninsula, it was an appeal to join hands to eliminate the danger of a nuclear war.

As Mr. Harada is a man of religion, rather than overstepping able to further demonstrate its diplomatic strengths. While the results of the party's work is seen as an extension of statecraft, it is also engaged from the perspective of ordinary people.

I should add that, in saying Mr. Ikeda's diplomatic efforts create a foundation for Komeito's diplomacy, this does not imply that he instructs the party. Rather, his efforts to pursue dialogue and to take action for peace are a strong spiritual inspiration for the members of the party.

Contributing to peace in East Asia

The following is not an example of Komeito's diplomacy, but it was an important event, which I would therefore like to touch upon.

An article in the March 10, 2016 edition of the *Seikyo Shimbun* left a deep impression on me. It was about a meeting between Minoru Harada, who succeeded Mr. Ikeda as Soka Gakkai president, and Kyungnam University President Park Jee Kyu, during the former's visit to South Korea. Many readers may have failed to notice it, as it was a short article. The meeting was quite significant, however.

As is well known, tensions on the Korean Peninsula have been high this year. On January 6, 2016, North Korea conducted an underground thermonuclear test, and in February it launched a ballistic missile. These events have led

Chapter 5 A Key Agent in Diplomacy

nations.

From my perspective as a former diplomat, Mr. Ikeda's diplomatic instincts are exceptional. It is my view that he was convinced even before he was appointed as president of the Soka Gakkai that it would become a world religion.

To develop a world religion, it is important to build harmonious relations with countries the world over. Diplomatic skills become vital for a top leader of such a religious organization. A world religion cannot be established without diplomacy. I believe Mr. Ikeda's diplomatic instincts were cultivated through his sense of responsibility as a leader of the Soka Gakkai and his determination to develop that organization into a world religion.

Regarding the significance of private diplomatic initiatives, Mr. Ikeda wrote in a Japanese-language dialogue he published with US political journalist and author Norman Cousins that, while diplomacy carried out by diplomats is important, so too is the diplomatic work done independently by others outside of government. Conventional state diplomacy, he noted, sees matters solely from the perspective of national interests; in contrast, citizen diplomacy represents the face of ordinary people, as opposed to the face of the nation.

On the foundation of this extensive network of diplomatic relations that Mr. Ikeda established, as well as that of the SGI network spanning 192 countries and territories, Komeito is diplomatic efforts.

I have said in the past that it is irrefutable that Japan's diplomacy has been greatly aided by Mr. Ikeda's private initiatives. In an article for the November 2007 issue of *Ushio* magazine, I gave the example of how the first Abe administration (2006-2007) made extensive use of the network built by Mr. Ikeda in reestablishing relations with China, which had deteriorated under the Koizumi administration.

As evidence of the extent to which Mr. Ikeda's diplomacy is valued, I also pointed out that when Premier Wen Jiabao of People's Republic of China visited Japan in April 2007, the only non-governmental figure he met with was Mr. Ikeda.

Another remarkable example of Mr. Ikeda's citizen diplomacy occurred during the strained period in US-Soviet and Sino-Soviet relations in 1974 to 1975, when he visited the US, China and Russia and met with Premier Zhou Enlai, Premier Alexei Kosygin and Secretary of State Henry Kissinger respectively, acting as a mediator to smooth over relations. He was able to extract from Kosygin during their meeting the assurance that the Soviet Union had no intention of attacking or isolating China, a commitment which he was then able to convey to Zhou Enlai when he visited China. This is an historic example of how a private citizen was able to break through an impasse in diplomatic relations between

The relationship between Iraq President Saddam Hussein and Al-Qaeda, which was another rationale given, was also found to be nonexistent. For these reasons, the second Iraq War was later condemned by the world for being a war without just cause. This makes Komeito's stance in opposing the use of military force within the Junichiro Koizumi administration—which supported US actions—all the more meaningful (although Kanzaki did concede that supporting the US in this mission was a painful but necessary choice that had to be taken by the Japanese government, given its position).

Synced with citizen diplomacy

The friendship developed with China over the years by Soka Gakkai President Ikeda contributed enormously to Komeito's diplomatic successes with that country. China "chose" Komeito as the pipeline for developing Sino-Japanese relations on the basis of the trust they had for Mr. Ikeda, who had been advocating the normalization of relations since the 1960s.

This is not only the case with China. Komeito's diplomatic efforts with Russia and South Korea for instance, are also founded on the private diplomatic efforts of Mr. Ikeda, who founded the party. In other words, Komeito's diplomacy is closely linked to and would not exist without Mr. Ikeda's

Komeito's presence in the coalition government also makes for a stronger and richer Japan-US relationship. In issues such as the Japan-US security treaty, if only hawkish LDP members are there to take the lead, relations with the US would become one-dimensional. Komeito acts as a balancing agent in such situations.

Komeito's response to the Iraq War in 2003 is an example of this role. As the US-led coalition, which included the United Kingdom, carried out its offensive against Iraq on the assertion that it was a terrorist country possessing weapons of mass destruction, Komeito stood firm within the ruling coalition in its opposition to the US and UK's use of military force. For instance, on March 3, 2003, on the eve of the invasion of Iraq, Komeito sent a delegation to the US. The Komeito chief representative at the time, Takenori Kanzaki, met with US Deputy Secretary of State Richard Armitage on the 4th at the US Department of State and strongly requested they reconsider the war option and make efforts toward a peaceful resolution (details of this are given in Chapter 17 of the *Chronicle*). Up until the last minute, Komeito strove through efforts in diplomacy with the US to protect peace.

It is widely known that the US's assertion that Iraq possessed weapons of mass destruction—their primary justification for the invasion—was later found to be untrue.

Chapter 5 A Key Agent in Diplomacy

premier since the formation of the second Abe administration.

It was the Komeito, in other words, who turned the deteriorating relations with China around, soon after the Abe administration was formed. This alone demonstrates the party's significance to Japan's diplomatic relations with China.

I would like to point out here, however, that the important role that Komeito has played in Japan's diplomacy isn't limited to relations with China. When too much focus is placed on Komeito's strong bond with China, it obscures the breadth of the party's influence. It has played an equally important role in diplomatic relations with Russia, South Korea, Middle Eastern countries and the United States.

In my dialogue with Yamaguchi, "What Komeito is thinking now," I stated:

> The party most respected by the Communist Party of the Soviet Union was Komeito. A leader of this party's international affairs division clearly stated, "Among Japan's political parties, Komeito is the one we need to value the most." … As a diplomat working in the former Soviet Union and then Russian Federation from 1988 to 1995, in my opinion, the role Komeito played in Japan's diplomatic relations with Soviet Union and Russia was immense.

Japan's control over the Senkaku Islands.

However, when the LDP-Komeito coalition was restored in December of that same year following a general election, Komeito Chief Representative Natsuo Yamaguchi took steps to improve relations between Japan and China. He visited China bringing with him a personal letter from Prime Minister Shinzo Abe. In Beijing, he met with Xi Jinping just prior to his appointment as President of the People's Republic of China. The Chinese leader remarked on the important role Komeito has played in building friendship between the two countries over the years and expressed his hope for continued interparty exchange. He also asked that best regards be conveyed to Prime Minister Abe, saying he "looked forward to further contributions toward a new Sino-Japanese relationship."

During his talks with Xi Jinping, Mr. Yamaguchi also proposed an exchange with Komeito's younger parliament members and sent delegates to China in the fall of 2013. In June the following year, the then Land, Infrastructure and Transportation Minister Akihiro Ota [and Komeito member] also visited China and met with a vice premier. This was the first time a cabinet member had met with a Chinese vice

---

1 Noda became prime minister in 2011 following the Democratic Party of Japan's victory in the 2009 House of Representatives election, ousting the LDP-Komeito coalition from power at the time.

Chapter 5   A Key Agent in Diplomacy

At the end of the chapter is this quoted statement by Takakazu Matsuda, an editorialist for the *Mainichi Shimbun*:

> The normalization of Sino-Japanese diplomatic relations was the result of Komeito's diplomatic efforts. Diplomatic negotiations are said to be the sole prerogative of the government. However, despite being in the opposition, Komeito played an immense role in normalizing relations.

As this assessment conveys, the first thing that comes to mind at the mention of Komeito and diplomacy is the party's contributions as regards relations with China. Its role as a bridge between the Japanese and Chinese governments in the process of the normalization of diplomatic relations is a particularly salient achievement that will shine in the party's history.

Needless to say, too, the strong bond Komeito has built with China since the 1970s and which it maintains until this day has been an enormous influence in strengthening and improving Sino-Japanese relations.

Other examples from recent years include: In September 2012, at the worst possible moment, just before the National Congress of the Communist Party of China (which was held that November), the Yoshihiko Noda cabinet[1] set back relations between the two countries when it nationalized

organization wishes to protect itself by not disclosing certain information to the public, actually publishing false information is risky, and, the larger an organization, the more apparent such dishonesty becomes.

The claim, then, that one cannot grasp the essence of the Soka Gakkai by reading public information is myopic. Public information is sufficient to make an elemental analysis.

Conversely, could one properly understand the Soka Gakkai by gathering up old denunciatory tabloid articles, or through information "leaked" by anonymous sources and individuals who have been expelled from the organization? That would surely only provide a distorted perspective.

This is why, even in criticizing Komeito or the Soka Gakkai, rather than using questionable sources, arguments should be based on public information. This is a vital precondition for presenting an accurate case.

More than just China policy

Chapter 7 of the *Chronicle*, "Laying the tracks for the restoration of Sino-Japanese diplomatic relations," deals with the issue of international diplomacy. It explores the significant role played by the Komeito in the normalization of China-Japan diplomatic relations in 1972, during the administration led by Kakuei Tanaka.

would be able to understand how Japanese politics is trending. The same could be said of trends in Japan's international diplomacy. In fact, one cannot discuss Japanese diplomacy without considering the efforts of Komeito and the Soka Gakkai.

This point is easily substantiated by a simple perusal of the *Komei Shimbun* and the *Seikyo Shimbun*, the newspapers of the party and the Soka Gakkai respectively. The problem is that the country is rife with critics who begrudge the effort to do even that, and who would opine on Komeito on the basis of the most superficial knowledge.

Incidentally, when I wrote "The Soka Gakkai and Pacifism," I based it solely on publicly published information. Much of the reference material was in fact articles that could be read on the *Seikyo Shimbun*'s website Seikyo Online or SOKAnet, the Soka Gakkai's official website. I did this so as to guarantee the verifiability of the sources. If readers want to verify the information I cited, they can simply read the original source online. This is important.

Some critics disapproved of my decision to use only public information, pointing out that one cannot truly understand the Soka Gakkai by simply reading the official public information it publishes.

I disagree. The larger any organization becomes, the more difficult it becomes for it to be publicly dishonest. Even if an rather than by his title of Honorary President of the Soka Gakkai.

As the Soka Gakkai develops as a world religion, so too does the role played by Komeito to become more global in scope. The value afforded the field of international diplomacy within Komeito is a reflection of this.

In a general sense, Komeito is known as a party strong on social welfare and education issues, rather than foreign policy. Even if it has gained a reputation for its policy work on social security initiatives, not many people would associate the party with efforts in diplomacy.

While it is true that no Komeito member has ever occupied the position of Minister of Foreign Affairs, diplomacy is not exclusively the role of that ministry, nor of the prime minister. In the fifty years since its formation, Komeito has carried out important diplomatic initiatives for Japan, and the significance of their role has only become greater since it formed a coalition government with the Liberal Democratic Party.

It is this diplomatic role, as reflected through the *Chronicle*, that I will explore in this chapter.

Public sources and verifiability

In Chapter 1, I expressed the opinion that as long as one observes the moves of Komeito and the Soka Gakkai, one

Chapter 5
A Key Agent in Diplomacy

Hiromi Takase, a candidate for the Fukuoka district constituency in the House of Councillors election this summer (2016), is a former diplomat. Hirotaka Ishikawa, a member of the House of Councillors from the Osaka district running for his second term, also served in the Ministry of Foreign Affairs and used to be a diplomat specializing in Middle Eastern diplomacy (Both were elected on July 10). It is no coincidence that many of the notable young Komeito members and candidates are experts in foreign affairs. This reflects the significance placed on diplomacy within Komeito.

One reason for this is the party's emphasis on global peace. Another, though, is that its supporting organization, the Soka Gakkai, is becoming recognized as a world religion.

An indication of this is the growing number of faith experiences of overseas Soka Gakkai International (SGI) members printed in the Soka Gakkai organ paper, *Seikyo Shimbun*, over the past year or two. Another is that it has become more common recently for the organization in Japan to refer to its top leader, Daisaku Ikeda, as SGI President,

Ikeda retreated by stepping down as president, but during the second priesthood issue, he won by gaining independence from the temple.

With regard to the "freedom of speech" incident, there had been no such victory in the "second round." However, with the *Chronicle* confronting the issue directly and stating that "we were in fact the victims of verbal abuse," Komeito was attempting to settle this long-pending issue once and for all. At the time of the incident, there was strong public prejudice against the Soka Gakkai and there was no choice but to make a tactical retreat. Now, however, some forty years later, understanding of the Soka Gakkai and Komeito has deepened and the foundation on which to settle this matter had been established.

There has been almost no formal reproach from the political world or the mass media regarding the *Chronicle*'s reference to the incident. With this, I believe that victory in the second round for Mr. Ikeda was realized at last.

---

1 The first of two incidents in which the priesthood of the Nichiren Shoshu Buddhist sect with which the Soka Gakkai was affiliated felt threatened by the growing influence of the lay movement and its leader. The key point of conflict stemmed from Ikeda's insistence in the essential equality of priests and lay believers; in way of diffusing tensions, he resigned as Soka Gakkai president in 1979.

Chapter 4 Confronting the "Freedom of Speech" Incident

We see here how, while apologizing, Mr. Ikeda clearly states that there was no intent whatsoever to obstruct the freedom of speech, and that the issue was contingent on how it was perceived.

His words, "continue . . . upholding the principle," imply that there was already a separation of politics and religion in place, and that the Soka Gakkai's support of Komeito is unproblematic under the constitution. Having said so, he declares that they will "continue as before to lend support" to Komeito.

In other words, Mr. Ikeda skillfully employed the art of rhetoric to say what needed to be said without being extreme. The speech, it could be said, is an example of a tactical retreat.

Looking at Mr. Ikeda's life, one can detect a pattern in this the act of making a tactical retreat in order to regroup and claim victory in the second round. Consider, for example, the Osaka incident, when Mr. Ikeda was wrongfully arrested. On recognizing the prosecutor's intent, he made a tactical retreat by admitting to the charges leveled by the prosecution as part of a dispassionate assessment of the power dynamic at play. However, in the court battle, which could be considered the "second round," he emerged victorious with a not-guilty verdict. The same happened with the Soka Gakkai's conflict with the priesthood.[1] During the first priesthood issue, Mr.

for Komeito to do.

The *Chronicle*'s chapter on the incident explains the history of the issue in detail, making starkly evident the truth that the Soka Gakkai and Komeito were the victims of violent speech.

At a general meeting of the Soka Gakkai on May 3, 1970, President Ikeda gave a lengthy speech on the issue. It was an explanation from the president himself in response to the criticisms of the Soka Gakkai raging across the nation.

Mr. Ikeda could have countered these criticism by saying the Soka Gakkai was the real victim. However, taking into account the state of public opinion, he chose the path of a tactical retreat by making the difficult decision to apologize.

The key parts are published in the *Chronicle*, but it is truly a remarkable speech so I will share an excerpt:

> We had absolutely no intent so insidious as obstructing the freedom of speech, yet our words and actions were seen as being obstructive and it is extremely regrettable and unfortunate that those involved felt pressured and that this was troubling the general public.
>
> We will continue to adhere to the way we operate, upholding the principle of separating the relationship between the Soka Gakkai and Komeito … Needless to say, the Soka Gakkai will continue as before to lend support at the party's main supporting organization.

publication work calling on the publisher and bookstores to ask them to reconsider their decision on handling this book. This was later criticized as being a form of oppression, but I disagree. Oppression is exercised by rulers or government institutions, such as state-run media outlets. It is illogical to use the term "oppression" in reference to the actions of a non-governmental organization such as the Soka Gakkai.

Furthermore, when the Soka Gakkai made their requests and protests, it didn't resort to violence or threats, or do anything illegal. Its actions were the natural response of a private organization on being informed of the release of a book containing baseless slanders against it, and calls to put an end to this were borne out of the wish to spare members from pain and undue prejudice.

And the contents of *I Denounce Soka Gakkai* were simply horrendous, filled with slanderous defamations bordering on hate speech. It compared the Soka Gakkai to the Nazis, calling them "bacteria that poisons the entire nation," "a parasitic scavenger feeding on the underbelly of democracy," and "a group of fanatics." In other words, the real victim of abuse was the Soka Gakkai. Nevertheless, the incident was exploited politically as a befitting rationale to attack the Soka Gakkai and Komeito. And it is still utilized to broadcast concerns relating to them. This is why tackling the negative image fomented by the incident in the *Chronicle* was the right thing

Matsuoka, "Discussing the Soka Gakkai," is devoted to this issue, and so the details of my view can be found there. However, I would like to share a few key points here.

"The freedom of speech" controversy refers to the incident which took place in 1969 when the Soka Gakkai demanded political commentator Hirotatsu Fujiwara cease his unfounded slanders following the publication of his book *I Denounce Soka Gakkai*. This developed into a major dispute, with the Diet and mass media claiming that this was a form of oppression and a violation of the freedom of speech and freedom of the press. The incident, by the way, is the term by which the Soka Gakkai and Komeito refer to the controversy, but generally it is known as the "obstruction of free speech and press incident."

I Denounce Soka Gakkai was published in November 1969, but posters promoting its release were displayed extensively in trains from as early as August. In December, a House of Representatives snap general election was held following rumors of an imminent dissolution that began around the summer. Mr. Fujiwara's book, was, therefore, clearly intended to undermine the results of the Lower House election that year.

This sequence of events led the Soka Gakkai to launch a protest, which included talks with Mr. Fujiwara prior to the book's release and Soka Gakkai members involved in

In the first place, the fact some media took issue with Komeito members having faith is absurd. This is a result of prejudice arising from a distorted idea of the separation of politics and religion.

German Chancellor Angela Merkel is the leader of the Christian Democratic Union and on numerous occasions has openly discussed her faith with the media. German President Joachim Gauck is a former Lutheran pastor (of the Evangelical Church in Germany). Nonetheless, the faith of state leaders is not an issue in Germany.

A teaching point for the future

Recently, I have had several opportunities to talk with men and women of the Soka Gakkai. I have been surprised to learn that many young members don't know about the "freedom of speech" incident. In some ways this is only natural, as this event took place over forty years ago.

However, the incident was critical for both Komeito and the Soka Gakkai and is still one of the causes of the negative image that dogs them. Even younger Gakkai members, then, should be aware of the background and the essence of this issue. In that sense, the *Chronicle*'s allocation of an entire chapter to it is significant.

A chapter of my dialogue with Buddhist philosopher Mikio

does it mention the two controversies. This further highlights the standard Komeito approach to these issues for the past forty odd years—to skirt them as far as possible.

To avoid these issues at this time in the *Chronicle*—which assuredly will be the key reference for any discussion on Komeito for many years—would have been to turn a blind eye to future trouble. And the book itself would have been a half-measure without much credibility.

Fortunately, the *Chronicle* avoided this fate, tackling the "freedom of speech" incident in Chapter 6 while dedicating Chapter 14 to a refutation of the criticisms of charges of its violation of the principle of the separation of politics and religion.

With these two chapters, the value of the *Chronicle* as the party's history increased manifold. Soon, a dialogue between Komeito Chief Representative Natsuo Yamaguchi and myself, "What Komeito is thinking now" will be released (April 2016). Mr. Yamaguchi devotes a quarter of the book to a frank discussion of his faith and religious beliefs. To publish a book right before the House of Councillors election in which the party's chief reveals himself as a Soka Gakkai member is unprecedented; Komeito's sincerity at this time in tackling its oversensitivity to the issue of the separation of politics and religion is unmistakable. And this all began with the *Chronicle*.

Chapter 4 Confronting the "Freedom of Speech" Incident

words, has only damaged the image of Komeito.

It is for this reason that I stressed in my 2014 book "Soka Gakkai and Pacifism" that Komeito and the Soka Gakkai should close the distance that separates them in a more visible way that's clear for even non-members.

And this is why I was so thrilled by the opening words of the foreword of the *Chronicle*, published shortly after, stating, "The Komeito was founded on November 17, 1964 at the initiative of the then Soka Gakkai President Daisaku Ikeda," along with a photograph of a young Mr. Ikeda on the frontispiece.

The effort to make the close relationship between Komeito and the Soka Gakkai more visible to the public had to be tackled together with the "freedom of speech" and association of politics and religion controversies. Since the "freedom of speech" incident has been the main cause for their oversensitivity regarding the separation of politics and religion, they couldn't correct the latter without confronting the former.

What would the effect have been, had the *Chronicle* not tackled these two issues while embracing Mr. Ikeda in the way it did in the book's foreword and on its frontispiece?

Komeito's official website has a section called "fifty years of the Komeito in pictures." Although it begins with the Soka Gakkai Culture Department's entry into politics, nowhere

Chapter 4

Confronting the "Freedom of Speech" Incident

I have discussed two respects in which *The Fifty-year Chronicle of Komeito* is novel: its acknowledgement of the contributions of the party's founder, Daisaku Ikeda, and, second, its direct confrontation of the issues stemming from the so-called "freedom of speech" incident and the controversy over the close association of politics and religion.

These two points are closely related. Over the past forty or so years, Komeito has, in my opinion, been hypersensitive about its relationship to the Soka Gakkai, overemphasizing its commitment to the separation of politics and religion and not even mentioning Mr. Ikeda as the party founder in its publications. In many ways, this is a response to the barrage of heavy criticisms Komeito and the Soka Gakkai received from the mass media and the political establishment over the "freedom of speech" incident.

But for non-Soka Gakkai members, the overemphasis on the separation of politics and religion has created the adverse impression that Komeito was dubiously attempting to conceal its relationship with the Soka Gakkai. This stance, in other

over those two hurdles with remarkable aplomb.

the 2023 "invoice system" in the accounting system, in order to accommodate the reduced tax rate, will further burden small- and medium-sized enterprises and sole proprietors. I do not agree.

Rather, the fact that the invoice system hasn't been adopted even thirty years after the introduction of consumption tax is an even greater problem. It is almost the same as the country saying to its citizens, "We'll leave it to a rough estimate, like the simple ledgers kept by merchants in the Edo and Meiji period, so just pay the taxes as you're told." This is not how a modern nation thinks.

It goes without saying that in this twenty-first century, corporations should keep accounts using double-entry bookkeeping and not old-fashioned ledgers.

Simple accounting software is readily available nowadays and a transition period is in place before the invoice system is implemented, so it is not an impossible request. It is in the best interests of smaller enterprises to take this opportunity to learn proper bookkeeping.

In any case, whether it be the issue of a lower tax rate for low-income citizens or the 2015 peace and national security legislation, I believe these were important hurdles that Komeito needed to be overcome at this time, five decades after its founding, when it is transforming into a full-fledged member of the ruling coalition. And Komeito has prevailed

was Komeito.

Furthermore, regarding the tax rate offset that is slated for adoption concurrently with the consumption tax hike, there are some who underestimate its impact saying, "It's only a difference of 2%" (10% consumption tax against 8% reduction in tax).[1] However, when considering the future, it can't possibly be said to be a matter of "only" anything. When we look at European countries that are more advanced as regards their consumption taxes, or considering the situation in Japan with its fast declining birthrate and rapidly aging population, it is unlikely the consumption tax would remain at 10% for long. It is highly probable that it would eventually be raised to 15%, or even 20%. In view of such eventualities it was extremely important that the framework to ease the tax hit on low-income earners be created now.

The reduced tax rate applying to all food items and the introduction of this program occurring alongside the consumption tax hike to 10%, can all be credited to the Komeito. And this feat will surely be validated in the future, when the consumption tax is raised even further.

The objection has been raised that the implementation of

---

1 As of this writing, the consumption (or sales) tax in Japan is 8% on all goods and services. The government decided in June 2016 to delay the increase in consumption tax until October 2019, at which time it will be raised to 10%. Komeito has been urging that the 8% rate remain in place, or offset, on eggs, milk and other basic necessities because studies have shown that low-income earners will be hardest hit if the tax is hiked by another 2%. (Editor)

loans. These are the people I term the "fiscally irresponsible needy," people who, for similar reasons, are unable to break out from the low-income demographic.

If the tax credit system that some political parties are promoting were to be adopted, these payments would probably be conducted trimonthly, not monthly—an inevitable consequence of the burden of paperwork it imposes on administrative bodies. In this case, three-month's worth of payment would be distributed to low-income earners every quarter. When this happens, the financially irresponsible among the low-income bracket would most likely burn quickly through the three-month's worth of payment. And there won't be another payment forthcoming just because they spent it all; government agencies would simply tell them that they alone are responsible for their spending habits.

To assert, then, that "tax credits are more beneficial for low income earners" demonstrates a lack of awareness of the realities of low-income earners.

Rather, easing even a little the daily expenditure of low-income citizens, for instance in their grocery purchases, would be a more genuinely helpful approach. Komeito, which, since its formation, has continued to support ordinary people and pay attention to social welfare, understood this point explicitly. The party that truly fought on the side of "the socially vulnerable" in the debate surrounding this tax issue

Protecting the socially vulnerable

I would like to take this opportunity to share my opinion on Komeito's efforts on the introduction of a program to reduce the tax hit on low-income citizens.

Among parties and intellectuals who object to this initiative, there are some who claim that tax credits combining refunds, such as cash credits and income tax adjustments, is a better plan. They argue that while the ruling coalition's program also somewhat benefit high-income earners, tax credits focus on benefiting low-income earners.

On the surface, this argument may seem correct. However, I believe this reasoning doesn't truly take the interests of the low-income demographic into consideration.

Among low-income earners, there are a large proportion of people who could be considered as the "fiscally irresponsible needy." This is a term that I have coined in reference to men and women who cannot or will not adhere to sound spending habits and, therefore, find themselves in recurring financial distress.

For example, there are people who can't properly allocate their monthly salary to their daily expenses for the month. They tend to spend money as it comes, unable to make their wages last until their next payday, living hand to mouth on

and "the penultimate" (*die Vorletzten*). The essential difference between the Komeito and JCP can be better understood from this viewpoint.

For JCP, politics is the ultimate. However, for Komeito, politics is the penultimate. Herein lies the fundamental difference between the two parties.

For Komeito, and also for Soka Gakkai members, politics, study, and work, are all penultimate things. The "ultimate" resides in religious truth.

Since politics isn't the ultimate end for Komeito, the party is able to compromise fittingly when required. "Compromise" may not give the right impression, but as the German chancellor Otto von Bismarck—nicknamed the "Iron Chancellor"—famously noted, politics is a product of compromise and equally, the art of the possible. Compromise is vital in politics. It could be said that the most important quality necessary for a politician is to know when to compromise.

However, for the JCP, politics is the ultimate, an end in itself. For this reason, they are unable to be flexible or to compromise. Their attitude of objecting to everything demonstrates how it is a party that can't compromise when needed.

religion of communism" (as historian Dr. Arnold J. Toynbee characterized that ideology).

JCP members, however, do not consider communism a religion, rather they believe it to be a universal science. Furthermore, there is a side to them that holds religion in contempt, following Marx's view that "religion is the opium of the masses." This is what makes them even nastier to deal with.

In Christianity, the concept of original sin—the doctrine of humanity's state of sin resulting from Adam and Eve's rebellion against God in the Garden of Eden—should serve as an important brake governing human behavior. It prevents people, in other words, from falling into the self-righteous belief that they are absolutely correct.

As I understand it, the concept of original sin doesn't exist for Soka Gakkai members, but the principle of the mentor-disciple relationship and the concept of their shared vow similarly act as governing constraint on behavior.

There are, however, no such limiters for believers in the "communist religion," and this is what makes the thought of them continuing to plunge ahead in their self-righteousness so frightening.

Dietrich Bonhoeffer, one of the most renowned Christian theologians of the twentieth century, examined reality through the perspective of the concepts of "the ultimate" (*die Letzten*) "people's coalition government"—a political partnership of opposition parties that seek to abolish the national security-related laws. This idea of a "people's coalition government" borrows from the phrase initially used by the Socialist Party of Japan (now Social Democratic Party) of a "national coalition government." The JCP previously termed it a "democratic coalition government" but has borrowed the SDPJ's term in its eagerness to become a central player in Japanese politics.

On January 4, 2016, JCP Chairman Kazuo Shii and other JCP members attended the opening of the ordinary Diet sessions. This was after sixty-nine years of absence. JCP, which disapproves of the emperor system, had not attended the opening session since 1947, citing the formal opening of the session by the emperor as deviation from his constitutional status. However, out of the blue, they decided to renege on this philosophy.

Possibly, the JCP members are unconsciously starting to feel anxious about the leading role that Komeito has begun to play in Japanese politics. This anxiety is materializing at the same time as are the feckless and desperate conciliatory attempts to overcome widespread public aversion to the JCP.

Why has the JCP built such strong sense of rivalry against Komeito to begin with? Fundamentally, it is because the JCP is a kind of a religious political party itself, serving "the amendment to the Soka Gakkai regulations. In a sense, these two events are like two sides of a coin. The amendment to the regulations represents the Soka Gakkai's opportunity to take flight to becoming a truly world religion, and the publication of the *Chronicle* similarly represents the Komeito soaring into the next phase of its existence, having come to the end of its developmental period. Having said that, I am not suggesting that these departures were some kind of coordinated plan by the Soka Gakkai and Komeito, but that their occurrence at the same time is an indication of developments in what you might call the "collective unconscious" of these organizations.

Key difference with JCP

When the LDP-Komeito coalition government came under heavy fire regarding the peace and national security legislation of 2015, the party that reaped the benefit by "fishing in troubled waters" was the Japan Communist Party (JCP).

The JCP is in some ways becoming a notable player in Japanese politics, growing into the second largest opposition party in both the House of Councillors and House of Representatives while also gaining influence at the local assembly level. This is a frightening thought.

Among the initiatives introduced by the JCP recently is the

Chronicle was to prepare for that day. For example, the *Chronicle* devotes one chapter each to the "freedom of speech" issue and criticism over the association of politics and religion, openly asserting that Komeito is not at fault and is strictly within its right under the constitution. These are the two issues that are still thorns in the side of the party and which it would like to bring closure to, ensuring the issues are not impediments when the time comes for a Komeito leader to take office.

I have repeatedly mentioned here that the *Chronicle* is unprecedented in the manner in which it clearly declares the contributions of party founder and Soka Gakkai Honorary President Daisaku Ikeda. This, I believe, is Mr. Yamaguchi's heartfelt hope to redress Komeito's oversensitivity to criticism over the separation of politics and religion that began with the "freedom of speech" incident and to finally move past these issues during his tenure.

Oddly enough, in November 2014, the same month the *Chronicle* was published, Komeito's supporting organization, the Soka Gakkai, announced an important amendment to its regulations. I will omit the details of the amendment but in a nutshell, the Soka Gakkai declared a complete separation from the Nichiren Shoshu sect of Buddhism.

I do not believe it was a coincidence that the publication of the *Chronicle* occurred in the same month as the

Chapter 3　Transition to Flight

with politics. This time the criticism was the standard criticism over policy, such as doubt over whether the three principles presented by the Komeito as conditions for the overseas deployment of the SDF would truly halt the exercise of the right of collective self-defense. The criticism was not of a mocking type, but was reproof that took Komeito seriously. This also shows how perception of Komeito has shifted.

I have often mentioned that if there is one thing on which I take issue with the Soka Gakkai, it is how the organization underestimates itself. The same could be said for Komeito. The party should have more confidence in the abilities that it has steadily cultivated over the past half century.

It is my opinion that within the next fifty years—that is, before the party's centennial anniversary—we will see the emergence of an administration led by a Komeito member. In other words, the day will come when a member of the Komeito will become prime minister.

I may be laughed at now for such a statement, but I am not indulging in fantasy. I say it with conviction, based on instincts developed through observing Japanese politics over many years: an administration led by the Komeito is a future reality that awaits us.

Moreover, I believe—though this is simply my conjecture—that Mr. Yamaguchi is also convinced of and truly anticipating such a future, and that another reason for publishing the continues to regard them in this manner will grossly misinterpret the political situation in Japan.

A future Komeito-led administration?

The first fifty years of Komeito until 2014, could be considered a long formative period.

Having now completed this phase in its development, the party has since 2015, entered a new period in which it willfully take flight.

After a half century of steadily climbing the stairs, Komeito has reached a landing of sorts. As such, the *Chronicle* is a groundbreaking work of history produced by Komeito members who have unconsciously grasped this reality.

There are many intellectuals in Japan who have intuitively recognized how the Komeito has soared in the past year or two. That is why the number of informed people who support the party is increasing. As someone with a strong relationship with the mass media, I can feel this change firsthand.

Saying so may prompt some to recall the media reports at the end of last year filled with negative commentary of Komeito regarding its handling of the 2015 peace and security legislation.

Most of that criticism, however, was of a different quality to the slanderous bashing of the past that had nothing to do legislative package on peace and national security measures. In it, Komeito Chief Representative Natsuo Yamaguchi addressed Mr. Abe and was able to elicit what was the only concrete example from him in which he stated, "We will not dispatch minesweepers to the Strait of Hormuz."

Minesweeping activities in the Strait of Hormuz in the Persian Gulf was a specific example the prime minister provided of Japan exercising the right of collective self-defense by its Self-Defense Force (SDF). On this matter, Mr. Yamaguchi used cold logic in his interpellation to corner Mr. Abe to concede that, "Given the state of current international affairs, it is not an issue that I imagine will take definitive form." Having made such a statement in public at the Diet, the prime minister was left with no choice but to relinquish any contingency dispatching minesweepers to the Strait.

There is no precedent of events unfolding in this way as a result of an inquiry within a ruling coalition. In truth, the Komeito's chief representative outperformed the president of the LDP in matters regarding international law and politics. This would have been unheard of a decade ago.

As this case has revealed, compared to when the LDP-Komeito coalition was first formed [in 1999], Komeito now has significantly more influence within the administration. The junior coalition partner is no longer the "snow clinging to the LDP's shoes," as the Japanese saying goes. Anyone who between the two parties on the introduction of a program that would ease the financial burden placed on low-income households if and when the consumption tax is raised to 10%. Initially, the LDP and Ministry of Finance argued that the reduced tax rate on food should be limited to fresh produce. Komeito, on the other hand, reasoned that it should also apply to processed foods which, ultimately, was the argument that prevailed.

During talks, Komeito was also able to keep the LDP and finance ministry at bay, quashing their idea of using the Social Security and Tax Number System to refund the reduction at a later date.

In the end, the LDP, including Prime Minister Abe, decided to accede to most of Komeito's terms regarding the specifics of the reduced rate. Some media outlets reported on this as the "Komeito sticking its nose into Ministry of Finance business." Admittedly, this would have been impossible ten years ago.

This kind of momentous transformation in Japanese politics has taken place over the past year or two. Komeito, in other words, is gaining significant influence, and not gradually, in small increments, but rapidly, as if sprinting up a flight of stairs.

The moment I felt this change keenly was on September 14, 2015, when I saw the live broadcast of the House of Councillors Special Committee hearings on the proposed

Chapter 3
Transition to Flight

In Chapter 1, I stated that the influence of Komeito within the administration led by Prime Minister Shinzo Abe is steadily increasing and that 2015 was a year in which Komeito became a key player in Japanese politics. I will delve a little deeper into these comments in this chapter. There are whispers to the effect that, recently, government officials in Kasumigaseki (the location of most ministry offices) are increasingly paying visits to Komeito members of parliament. These officials clearly recognize that the party has gained considerable influence in the past two years.

In the past, Komeito was the party on the forefront of social welfare issues. Yet, even after the formation of the LDP-Komeito coalition, core national issues such as national security and the tax system were under the exclusive jurisdiction of the LDP, giving Komeito limited influence.

However, that dichotomy is being overturned in recent years. Komeito is now a key player on such issues and is standing its ground against the LDP.

What is particularly symbolic of this trend has been debate

Komeito has always intended, since its formation, to "reform the system from within," and joining the coalition government, as we've seen in recent years, was inevitable.

Only after reading the "Struggles against authority" section of Mr. Ikeda's "My Personal History" can the *Chronicle* be understood in greater depth.

destroyed; nor did he turn Komeito into a dissident party.

Following the Osaka incident, Mr. Ikeda's thoughts most likely ran along the lines of: *There is still has such limited understanding of the Soka Gakkai among the establishment. This is where the discrepancy arises. We need to broaden awareness of the Soka Gakkai.*

Then what should be done? We must make "comrades" within the state power structures—not by enlisting them but by growing the number of Soka Gakkai members in government who share the same values. This will take time, but it won't take a century. It could be accomplished within twenty-five years. They could then reform the nation from inside the system.

I surmise these were the thoughts of young Mr. Ikeda.

And now, sixty years later, Soka Gakkai members have steadily emerged as government officials, judicial officials and legislators to the extent that Komeito now holds a vital position within the ruling coalition. This has nothing to do with the kind of idle gossip to the effect that "the Soka Gakkai is planning to dominate Japan," which we used to see smeared across tabloid magazines. Rather the Soka Gakkai is endeavoring to realize a grand vision of human revolution to "reform the nation through the reformation of people within the government." In other words, it is an endeavor of deconstructing the dangers of state authority.

advance together with the people."

The sentence ends here but I interpreted it to imply the continuation, "For this reason, I established the Komeito." I say so because earlier in the same section, he writes, "Komeito is a party that I founded, but currently, there is a distinct separation of politics and religion. In any case, I have great expectations for the party to contribute to the people of Japan and to realize a political agenda for social welfare."

In this essay that was written just five years after the "freedom of speech" incident, it was necessary for Mr. Ikeda to be cautious when referring to his relationship to Komeito. Hence his choice of words. However, to my way of thinking, this is a very important sentence which reveals Mr. Ikeda's sentiments in founding the party.

After being wrongfully arrested during the Osaka incident, Mr. Ikeda underwent harsh interrogation and experienced firsthand the brutality of state authority. This inspired his determination to fight against the unjust exercise of power, but the fact that this did not push him toward conflict with the establishment is a testament to his distinguished leadership.

Refuting the state or railing against national government officials—prosecutors, judges and others—is futile and results only in a kind of immature anti-authoritarianism, an irrational hostility toward the establishment. Mr. Ikeda did not follow that path, casting state authority as something to be

Chapter 2 Komeito as a Party of the Masses

Soka Gakkai's move into politics. The section is titled, "Struggle against authority". Here, Mr. Ikeda reflects on the "Osaka Incident" (1957), when he was baselessly accused of and arrested for election fraud, to which a court found him innocent of all charges.

Mr. Ikeda points out that the Osaka Incident was a form of oppression triggered by the victory of three Soka Gakkai Culture Department candidates in the House of Councillors election the previous July.

"It is true that at the time, there were attempts to inhibit the Soka Gakkai as its growth became more salient," he wrote. "Naturally, it follows that the bigger the waves, the greater the resistance."

Mr. Ikeda, then a young man, had spearheaded the campaign in the Osaka electoral district (referred to in the Soka Gakkai as the Osaka Campaign), achieving a miraculous victory and spawning newspaper headlines to the effect that the impossible had been achieved. The underlying strength of the Soka Gakkai was now revealed to all. This is likely the reason Mr. Ikeda became a target.

In "Struggle against authority," after clearly explaining the sequence of events during the Osaka Incident up until his not-guilty verdict, Mr. Ikeda writes: "In the depths of my heart, I could not help but to vow to spend my lifetime protecting people who suffer at the hands of unjust authority and to understand this intrinsic religious rationale better than most as practitioners of faith themselves.

This name change would be worldwide news, resulting in a major improvement to Komeito's image, since the party would be responsible for correcting the Foreign Affairs Ministry's unjust refusal of the request made by the Vatican. It would also give the impression that Komeito not only engages in work that will benefit the Soka Gakkai but truly respects and values religion as a whole.

It is a small yet significant reform that I hope Komeito would undertake, even if only to demonstrate its strength and meaningful role as a religious political party.

Reforming the system from within

A recommended supplementary work for better understanding of the *Chronicle* is Mr. Ikeda's book, "My Personal History".

The book is a long-running popular serialization in *The Nikkei* business daily, and when Mr. Ikeda was featured in this column in 1975, his submissions were compiled and published as a book. It is a very worthy autobiography. Just recently, a new edition of this book was published and it is an important read, especially for people who may not already be familiar with it.

In it, there is a section which comments firsthand on the

Chapter 2 Komeito as a Party of the Masses

to change the way the name of Georgia, a country in the South Caucasus region, was written in Japanese.

Georgia did not undergo any change in government that resulted in the country changing its name. The change in the registered name was a result of numerous requests made to the Japanese Government, such as by the Georgian President to Prime Minister Shinzo Abe in person during the former's visit to Japan.

As this demonstrates, if the government is willing, registered names—even those of a country—can readily be changed, and there should be no reason to refuse the change in title of the pope. Given the willingness, this could easily be accomplished.

My suggestion to Komeito, therefore, is take the lead on enacting a bill that will allow the name of both the pope and the Apostolic Nunciature to reflect their correct titles. Making this change would not inconvenience anyone; I cannot see any party opposing it. In fact, I imagine the bill would pass without issue. I also imagine the implications of such a change would be quite significant, improving relations between the Catholic community and Japan considerably.

When proposing such a bill, I suggest Komeito stress the reason as "wanting as a political party to respect the rationale intrinsic to a given religion." I believe it would be an apt argument to make for Komeito members in that they should the name of a diplomatic establishment in Japan is permitted except in special circumstances, such as when a country changes its name owing to an incident such as a coup d'état.

Tentatively translated, the official website of Catholic Bishops' Conference of Japan writes on this issue as follows:

> When Japan and the Vatican established diplomatic relations, the standard translation at the time [was inappropriate] so the Apostolic Nunciature in Japan was also mistakenly registered in Japanese as such rather than [using the correct character]. Unless the nation undergoes a change in government that results in a change to the name of that nation, it appears that the name registered under the Japanese government cannot be changed.

Since then, the name of the Apostolic Nunciature in Japan has remained inappropriately named and public television broadcaster NHK（Japan Broadcasting Corporation）also continues to use this title.

Personally, I always make sure to use the correct title in my writings. Some media outlets have started to adopt the term as well, but the incorrect title is still more commonly used.

Some may have been puzzled by the Foreign Affairs Ministry's statement regarding the inability to change a nation's registered name, seeing that in April 2015 a bill was enacted

To illustrate, there is one idea that I propose to the Komeito which could be easily carried out, if the party was willing to do so.

In the Japanese media, the Pope, or the Bishop of Rome, the leader of the worldwide Catholic Church (currently Pope Francis, the 266th pontiff), is referred to by two names, one of which is incorrect. The reason it is wrong is because it contains the Chinese character for "king" in the secular world and so is inappropriate for referring to the pope. The term is incorrect on another count because it also contains the character for the "law" (dharma) in Buddhism—a strange word to be used in reference to the supreme leader of the Catholic Church.

The Catholic Bishops' Conference of Japan, the central body of Catholic churches in Japan, has in fact expressed its displeasure at this term. In 1981, when the then Bishop of Rome Pope John Paul II visited Japan, a request was made to the Japanese government to standardize the title by using its most appropriate Japanese term. In addition, a request was made for the name of the Apostolic Nunciature in Japan (Embassy and Consulate General of Vatican in Japan), situated in Chiyoda Ward, Tokyo, to be changed in Japanese to reflect this correct title.

However, the Japanese government (the Ministry of Foreign Affairs) denied the request, stating that no change to

used when religious groups in Japan wanted to enter politics. Lacking the organizational strength to establish a party on their own, they would support parties such as the LDP and in return, would receive political benefits. Currently too, this is the way in which new religious groups typically enter the political arena.

Simply put, Komeito is the only religious political party in Japan that was able to firmly establish their political authority on their own and without resort to this tactic.

Admittedly, the formation of a political party by any other religious group would be of no interest to me. It is because Komeito is a party based on Nichiren Buddhism that I find it interesting. Although it is a party grounded in religion, Komeito as a mass-based political party cannot concentrate its efforts solely on religious policies. This goes without saying. However, I believe Komeito could have a much more straightforward embrace of its identity as a religious political party.

Earlier, I stated that Komeito tended to be overly sensitive to criticism regarding the separation of politics and religion after the events of the so-called "freedom of speech" incident and that I am pleased the party has revised this tendency in the *Chronicle*. That is all the more why I hope Komeito will boldly show its true colors in government as a political party based on religious principles.

political situation of modern Japan.

In his work, Marx offers an insight that, to paraphrase, goes along the lines of, "If there is no party representing the 'part' to which one belongs, then people will be ensnared by the party that goes against their interests." This was the case in Japan until the appearance of Komeito. People faced the dilemma of having to choose a party to vote for even though there was none that would speak out for them.

In these circumstances, Komeito endeavored to become, as stated in its Party Platform, "a mass-based political party which will embrace people from all social strata," and emerged as the first political party to represent the most prevalent "part" of society—the so-called common people.

Strength as a religious political party

What strikes me most is the fact that this mass-based party, Komeito, emerged in the form of a religious political party.

There is a term called the French Turn. It is something often seen in the New Left and it refers to the tactic employed by an organization that faces difficulty expanding independently. The tactic is to first join forces with existing parties or political organizations and gradually develop influence from within.

Prior to Komeito, the French Turn was a tactic commonly

The word for *sei-to* in English is "political party." For example, *Jiyu-minshu-to* is "Liberal Democratic Party" and is abbreviated as LDP.

The word "party" comes from "part," meaning a segment of a whole. In other words, political parties are not a representative of society as a whole, rather they represent one "part" or segment of society. Political parties exerting themselves as representative of a "part" is what democracy is about.

However, in Japan, until the emergence of the Komeito, there was never a political party that represented the majority "part" known as the masses.

For much of the nation's postwar history, the two major parties were the LDP and the Japan Socialist Party (JSP). The LDP was an advocate for the financial industry and large corporations, while the JSP was primarily a spokesperson for the labor unions. There was no single party that represented people who belonged neither to large corporations or labor unions (for instance, shop owners, housewives, etc.). Such people were left on the sidelines of politics to fend for themselves.

Amongst Karl Marx's writings is an essay called *The Eighteenth Brumaire of Louis Napoleon*. It is an analysis of the process leading up to the coup d'état of French Emperor Napoleon III, and I find it an instructive comparison to the

The speech was given at the first national convention of the PFCD on September 13, 1962, where Mr. Ikeda was the guest speaker:

> …I hope that, as politicians and as leaders, you will strive until the end of your days to stay directly connected to the people. I also hope that you will never grow self-important just because of your political standing, isolating and distancing yourself from the people, and that you will never rest on your laurels, hiding behind this political organization. I want you to speak with the people, fight for the people, and die among the people. It is my fervent wish that you, the members of the Komei Political Federation, will live out your lives fulfilling your responsibility to work for the happiness of all.[1]

These words, according to the *Chronicle*, "…were stipulated as a basic guideline and announced as the party's platform during the inaugural meeting two years later when the Komeito was formed." And indeed they have been cherished as the party's defining point of embarkation for the past half century.

I would also like to share my views on the meaning of "together with the people."

---

[1] Daisaku Ikeda, *The New Human Revolution*, (Santa Monica: World Tribune Press, 2003), vol. 9, pp. 306-07

of the book becomes clearer. This is a reading technique that I derived on my own.

If I were to hold a book club meeting for Soka Gakkai members on the *Chronicle*, I would begin by asking the participants to highlight all of Mr. Ikeda's words and carry the discussion forward with reference to those highlighted areas.

Similarly, here I would also like to proceed by calling attention to Mr. Ikeda's words from time to time.

First in Japan to represent the masses

The *Chronicle* does not address Komeito's history only from the time of the party's formation (on November 17, 1964) but devotes a chapter to the preceding events of the Soka Gakkai Cultural Department's foray into politics, in particular the period of the Political Federation for Clean Government (PFCG).

This description of Komeito's history dating back to the beginning of the Soka Gakkai's moves into politics is another unprecedented feature of the *Chronicle*.

Again, in the first chapter, "Prehistory," great emphasis is placed on Mr. Ikeda's words. Particularly, the speech that gave rise to what has become the perennial slogan of Komeito, "a political party for, of and by the people," is quoted at length.

Chapter 2

Komeito as a Party of the Masses

As I wrote in the preceding chapter, what makes *The Fifty-year Chronicle of Komeito* (*Chronicle* for short) groundbreaking is that it clearly establishes Soka Gakkai Honorary President Daisaku Ikeda's significance to the party.

This is not so only in the Foreword, which I examined earlier. Mr. Ikeda's words are cited throughout the book and it is made clear to the reader that the party founder has keenly followed the development of Komeito.

In my copy of the *Chronicle* I have highlighted all the places where Mr. Ikeda's words are cited. This makes it very easy to see at a glance where in the book his words appear. This is a little habit I developed in my days studying theology.

In copies of the Bible published abroad, the words of Jesus Christ are sometimes set in a different font, such as Gothic, or written in red, so that they can be easily referenced. Following this example, in the two-volume New Testament that I published (Bunshun Shinsho Publishing), and for which I also wrote a commentary, I set Jesus's words in Gothic font.

By highlighting the words of the key person, the structure

ruling coalition. Some might characterize this transformation and Komeito's collaboration in the coalition government as a deterioration and corruption, but I disagree. Rather, I believe that Komeito, in joining the ruling coalition, has enabled the party to achieve great growth. I will examine this idea in an upcoming chapter.

coalition gained power, Komeito was targeted on the politics and religion issue. Under these circumstances, had they published a history book candidly addressing the importance of Mr. Ikeda, it would have been used as a weapon to attack them.

A topic that would have caused an uproar twenty years ago is no longer an issue and raises nary an eyebrow today. This transformation demonstrates that in the past decade or so since the LDP-Komeito coalition was formed, the public's perspective of Komeito has changed significantly.

Even looking at the past year alone, the growing presence of Komeito in politics compared to the past is obvious to anyone. From debates around the legislation on peace and national security that took place from the spring to fall, to the adoption of easing the tax hit on low-income citizens at the end of the year, there was almost not a single day that passed without the mention of Komeito in the mass media.

That is not to say these were all positive reports. However, it was certainly a year in which Komeito became a key player in Japanese politics on such core issues as national security and the tax system. This would have been unimaginable twenty years ago, when Komeito was able to take the lead only in select areas such as social welfare and education.

As public perception has changed, so too has Komeito itself, in the process of gaining experience as a party in the burnt child dreading fire.

If the criticisms regarding the association of politics and religion once aimed at Komeito and the Soka Gakkai were legitimate, then the accounts within the *Chronicle* would have been frowned upon and brought up in Diet sessions to attack Komeito. That this has not happened is corroboration of the fact that such criticisms were made simply for the sake of political expedience.

More than the absence of criticism on this point, is the fact that there was almost no backlash from the public over the *Chronicle* itself. This could also indicate that Komeito, given its longstanding overreaction to the issue of separation of politics and religion, had been fearful of an illusion. When Komeito courageously stepped forward to reveal to the public its close relationship to Mr. Ikeda, the public rather unexpectedly accepted the fact with ease.

Protagonist in Japanese politics

What would have happened had a similar history been published twenty years ago presenting Mr. Ikeda's influence in such a forthright manner?

When Komeito marked its thirtieth anniversary in 1994 it was then part of a coalition of non-LDP parties (the Tsutomu Hata Cabinet) following the LDP's loss of power. When that

A groundbreaking work

The *Chronicle* devotes an entire chapter on the "freedom of speech" incident and refutes the numerous criticisms it engendered. Another chapter is dedicated to the criticisms regarding the close association of politics and religion and clearly contends that Komeito's participation in government does not violate the constitutional prohibition against the unification of church and state.

These positions are in exact alignment with my own views. At this fiftieth anniversary milestone, Komeito is finally rectifying its excessive sensitivity to the issue of separation of politics and religion and is asserting the vital role that Mr. Ikeda serves in the party's genesis. In that sense, the *Chronicle* is a fresh and innovative work that I believe will be a key reference for any future discussion on Komeito and the Soka Gakkai.

More than a year has passed since the *Chronicle* was published but criticism of its content (including that regarding the association of politics and religion) has been close to nil as far as I can see. This fact alone proves that public understanding of Komeito has grown, and also that in its past the party has been overly sensitive to the issue of separation of politics and religion—a case, as the saying goes, akin to a underground bedrock—ensuring the buildings were earthquake resistant—when in fact they had not.

This falsification problem had not yet been uncovered during the time Mr. Yamaguchi wrote the foreword for the *Chronicle*. Coincidence though it may be, rereading the foreword has reminded me of the current reports on the falsification of piling data and proves how appropriate the metaphor of a construction pile is for Komeito's political role.

If we compare political parties to buildings, then the pile driven deep into the bedrock is the philosophy that guides their political activities. Komeito, though, in my view, is the only party in Japan with such a pile—a firm philosophy.（It could be argued that the JCP has communism as their foundation, but I will comment on the essential differences between JCP and Komeito in another chapter.）

Other parties may appear to be magnificent buildings but they lack the philosophy that serves as a central column. This is why they constantly fluctuate, being "swayed by transitory trends or fads" and "oscillating to curry favor or resorting to flattery."

The reference to Komeito as "the lifeline of Japanese politics" and "a column driven deep into the ground" is indicative of Mr. Yamaguchi's immense pride in his party.

Politics sans guiding philosophy is rootless

Let me quote another noteworthy passage from the *Chronicle*'s foreword:

> There are scholars who regard Komeito as "the lifeline of Japanese politics" or "a column driven deep into the ground." This most likely is intended as praise for Komeito's stance as a political party that exercises power consistently without being swayed by transitory trends or fads. We neither oscillate to curry favor nor resort to flattery. Even during times of political ambivalence, Komeito remains unswerving and stands firm.

"A column driven deep into the ground" indicates the aforementioned philosophy, "The welfare and wellbeing of humanity is our end-value over all others." Komeito is a party that has the "column" of humanism based on Mr. Ikeda's philosophy and Nichiren Buddhism driven deeply at its very center.

Ironically, the problem of falsifying data on support columns in the construction of condominium buildings has recently become hot topic in Japan. Data was falsified to claim that these columns, or "piles," had penetrated the of life.

The quoted passage could be said, then, to be a condensation of Mr. Ikeda's philosophy of humanism. Also, the words, "a message carried into the twenty-first century" is clearly in reference to *Choose Life*, the famous dialogue between the historian Arnold Toynbee and Mr. Ikeda. The foreword, then, also implies that the ideals and philosophy of the party's founder, Mr. Ikeda, are at the foundation of the present-day Komeito.

Komeito has always been perceived as a centrist party. This could suggest that they are neither clearly on the left nor the right, though there is often the cynical implication that they are uncommitted and willing to shift in accordance with the prevailing political winds.

The centrist path to which Komeito aspires, however, is not one of such shallow views. For them centrism means holding fast to the ideal of "the welfare and wellbeing of the people." This is the core value that does not oscillate either left or right, regardless of circumstance, nationalism or ideology.

The foreword expresses clearly and concisely the true meaning of "centrism." I believe it was written by Chief Representative Yamaguchi, and in it, he offers a succinct and eloquent expression of the founder's philosophy, enabling the reader to realize that he, before being a legislator, is himself a practitioner of faith with solid morals and values.

The era is said to be converging towards centrism, although this doesn't simply mean that the distance between the left and the right has shrunk. What has become starkly evident in the post-Cold War period is was that people do not exist for the sake of the government or ideologies. The welfare and wellbeing of humankind is our end-value over all others. Whatever principles, structure or system—be it nationalism, ideology, or capitalism—should they not all be for the sake of serving the people? That is the conclusion that the twentieth century—a century of war and revolution—has brought us to, a message that humanity has supposedly carried into the twenty-first century. This is what is implied in the phrase, convergence toward centrism.

What does this passage imply? Conceivably it is that Komeito aspires to and upholds a set of values that is foundational to its political activities that is superior to any other principle, structure or system, whether it be nationalism, ideology, or capitalism.

This value is made clear in the foreword, "The welfare and wellbeing of humanity is our end-value over all others." People's lives inherently possess a supreme and irreplaceable worth. This is more than the mere sentimentalism of saying, for instance, that "a person's life is the most precious thing in the world." The phrase in the foreword reflects the Soka Gakkai's firmly held philosophy of humanism and the sanctity

party's founding. Moreover, the foreword by the current Komeito Chief Representative, Natsuo Yamaguchi, begins with this passage:

> The Komeito was founded on November 17, 1964 at the initiative of the then Soka Gakkai president, Daisaku Ikeda. The party, marking its fiftieth anniversary this November 17 (2014), has continued to actively engage in activities to promote public welfare based on the guideline of the founder, a political party for, of and by the people.

My impression is that the wording of this opening phrase has been carefully considered. By this, I mean that this phrase clearly states that the party was founded by the president of the Soka Gakkai, and that the principle of a political party for, of and by the people was established by Mr. Ikeda.

In other words, the idea of *obutsu myogo*[2] that had disappeared from the Komeito's platform has now reemerged in this foreword without reference to that particular phrase. This is what I mean by the foreword being bold yet carefully constructed.

The foreword also states as follows:

---

[2] Establishing the dignity of life and the spirit of Buddhist compassion at the core of culture and all human endeavors.

public. To outsiders, it seems that the Soka Gakkai and Komeito are trying to hide their relationship, which makes them appear disingenuous.

This is why I stated in my book, "Soka Gakkai and Pacifism" (Asahi Shinsho), "Komeito and Soka Gakkai should come together in a way that is more visible for others."

In any case, religious political parties are not uncommon in other countries, as can be seen with Germany's ruling party, the Christian Democratic Union (CDU). Even prior to the unification of East and West Germany, the CDU had a presence in East Germany, a socialist country that identified itself as atheistic. From a Judeo-Christian worldview, political life cannot ultimately be separated from religion.

The same is true for the Soka Gakkai, based on Nichiren Buddhism.

In any event, participation in politics by religious groups in itself does not violate the principle of separation of politics and religion as set out in the Constitution. Criticisms leveled against the Soka Gakkai and Komeito for mixing politics and religion are doubly distorted for being made simply for the sake of argument. I believe, therefore, that Komeito should be more vocal about the fact that it was founded by Daisaku Ikeda, on the values rooted in Nichiren Buddhism.

Regardless, *Chronicle*'s frontispiece prominently features a photograph of Mr. Ikeda in his youth at the time of the

Bold yet circumspect

What makes the *Chronicle* so extraordinary is that it firmly establishes Soka Gakkai Honorary President Daisaku Ikeda as the party's founder.

One might argue that there is nothing unusual about the party proclaiming its founder in a book about its history. However, this has not always been a simple matter for Komeito and the Soka Gakkai. Since the 1970s, Komeito has avoided mention of Mr. Ikeda as its founder out of concern over criticisms that it violates the principles of the separation of church and state.

For instance, the party's timeline on its official website still begins with the establishment of the Political Federation for Clean Government (Komeito's predecessor) and does not mention prior moves of Soka Gakkai's into the political arena.

It appears the damage caused during the so-called "freedom of speech" incident when the Soka Gakkai and Komeito came under heavy fire in the court of public opinion, has made them overcautious, a case of once bitten, twice shy.

However, its own excessive emphasis on the separation of politics and religion[1] has invoked a sense of doubt among the

---

[1] In Japan, the term is used in lieu of "separation of church and state."

power. In this sense, the party's movements cannot be predicted based on preconceived political logic. This is what makes Komeito hard to read and is why it is necessary to follow the party and the Soka Gakkai.

Moreover, as we can see with recent moves to reduce the tax burden on low-income households, the presence of Komeito within the Abe Administration is steadily increasing.

For a long time, since the formation of the LDP-Komeito coalition in 1999, Komeito has been ridiculed as being a sheep to the LDP—the perennial "giver" in a give-and-take relationship. However, Komeito, the minority partner in the coalition government, has now reached a point in which the party is able to force LDP, the majority partner, to make concessions. I predict this shift will persist and Komeito will continue to play a key role in Japanese politics.

This essay is an exploration of my opinion on the significance of Komeito's presence and the roles it should play in the future.

The most suitable reference in this endeavor is the *Chronicle* released by the party's historiography committee. This is an official history published in November 2014, to commemorate the fiftieth anniversary of the party's formation.

Instead of studying the *Chronicle* clause by clause, my aim is to examine its essence in order to probe the past and present of the party.

Japan could be considered an unchanging constant.

The direction of LDP is eminently predictable. The same can be said of the Japanese Communist Party (JCP). It is also clear that the DPJ has dissipated, resembling the random, incoherent movements of particles in Brownian motion. The former Japan Innovation Party and their associates may believe their work is worthwhile, yet they struggle day in and day out for what is inconsequential to Japan as a whole.

None of these political parties has sufficient influence to affect the overall development and direction of society; only Komeito has the potential to do so.

This is not simply to say that because of its size Komeito has a decisive influence in the House of Representatives and Councillors. Rather, Komeito is the only party that can bring about change in the fundamental framework of Japanese politics.

In Japan, Komeito is the only political party based on religious principles that has actual political authority. In other words, other parties merely operate within the realm of secular authority, constantly entering into or ending alliances and distributing power.

Only Komeito has the ability to take a bird's-eye-view of politics from a perspective that transcends secular matters and that can revitalize politics. It is able to bring reason to bear based on values that transcend the expedient logic of

Chapter 1

Komeito — A Deeply Driven Column

When contemplating present-day Japanese politics and forecasting the future, what I take most seriously into consideration are the activities of the Komeito Party and its supporting lay Buddhist organization, the Soka Gakkai. I could go so far as to say that as long as we observe the moves of Komeito and Soka Gakkai, we will understand political trends.

One reason for this is the situation that arose when the second Shinzo Abe Administration was established, a situation in which one strong party, the ruling Liberal Democratic Party (LDP), holds power amidst numerous weak parties.

Since it was ousted in 2012, the Democratic Party of Japan (DPJ) has waned and a "two-party system" no longer exists in Japan. Any so-called opposition party that can influence government has vanished and the only real political power able stop the LDP from spiraling out of control is Komeito, which could be called the opposition within the ruling party.

Further, with the exception of Komeito, political parties in destiny of Japan and the world through their work in politics. It is my hope that Japanese politics in the twenty-first century will evolve with Komeito as a core driver.

——December 10, 2016
Masaru Sato

Foreword

its platform when the party was formed two years later.

For the past half century, Komeito has adhered firmly to Mr. Ikeda's guideline. What is most important now, I believe, is to gain an understanding of Komeito based on a correct perspective of the principle of the separation of politics and religion, as Mr. Yamaguchi has indicated.

I am neither a member of the Komeito nor their supporting organization, the Soka Gakkai. I am a Christian, belonging to the United Church of Christ in Japan (UCCJ), the largest Protestant denomination in the country. I am not affiliated with any specific political party. However, being a Christian doesn't impinge in any way on my interactions with Komeito representatives or their supporting Soka Gakkai members. The principle of the separation of politics and religion is firmly held by Komeito. The party can be trusted because it is managed by professional politicians who share the same values as the Soka Gakkai, which cherishes peace, life and humanity. And while Komeito has been criticized for ostensibly pandering to authority or "tainting its trademark of peace," I admire its continuing exertions amidst political realities to "speak with the people, fight for the people, and die among the people."

My intention in this book is to analyze the *Chronicle* in order to demonstrate the reality that Komeito members, adhering to worthy values, are greatly transforming the

Komeito is currently endeavoring to correct this erroneous view.

In a book I co-authored with Mr. Yamaguchi in 2016, he states, "The separation of politics and religion set out in the Constitution of Japan is not a principle that prohibits certain religious groups from participating in political activities. The correct understanding of the principle of the separation of politics and religion is that the state should neither favor nor condemn any particular religion."[1] I am in complete agreement with Mr. Yamaguchi's comment.

Significantly, moreover, in its official history, *The Fifty-year Chronicle of Komeito: With the People* (hereinafter *Chronicle*), published in November 2014 to commemorate the party's golden anniversary, Komeito described the circumstances under which Soka Gakkai President Daisaku Ikeda established the party. The second page of this book's frontispiece shows a photograph of Mr. Ikeda, with the caption: "Komeito Founder Daisaku Ikeda".

In his speech at the Komei Political Federation's first national convention on September 13, 1962, Mr. Ikeda stated that Komeito representatives should "speak with the people, fight for the people, and die among the people." His words were adopted as the party's fundamental guideline and defined

---

[1] Masaru Sato and Natsuo Yamaguchi, "What Komeito is thinking now," (Tokyo: Ushio Shinsho, 2016), pg. 22

are in fact fulfilling that responsibility in the political arena. Therefore, to continue fully supporting the party will lead to the de facto maintenance of peace.

Outwardly, the Democratic Party of Japan has strongly opposed the right of collective self-defense but inwardly, the majority of its members are essentially in support of that right. Their objection is made purely from a political perspective. Komeito, based on their humanistic and pacifist values, is against the right of collective self-defense as it is fully defined, which exceed the scope of the right to individual self-defense acknowledged in the Constitution of Japan. That is why Komeito can be trusted. (September 25, 2015, *Komei Shimbun*)

I used the term "existential pacifists" but what is important to note is that Komeito is a political party of clearly defined values. And it is Komeito's supporting body, the Soka Gakkai, that plays the important function of enabling Komeito to shape those values. As I discuss in some detail in these pages, after the so-called "freedom of speech" incident in the 1970s, it became almost a taboo to speak in public about Komeito and Soka Gakkai's relationship. In addition, intellectuals and the mass media incorrectly interpreted the separation of politics and religion to mean that religious organizations could not have any involvement whatsoever in politics.

reality, such steadfast efforts to eliminate concerns one at a time generate far greater influence than organizing large-scale demonstrations.

People in power have a tendency to interpret the world to fit their wishes by conveniently disregarding verifiability and objectivity. On the other hand, Komeito possesses a genuine aptitude for logic and realism based on humanistic and pacifist values. The task ahead for Komeito is to think objectively, logically as well as realistically when a specific security issue arises, and protect peace by interpreting the legislation in accordance with the 2015 cabinet decision.

——What role should Komeito assume from now?

Sato: Komeito's role has shifted somewhat since talks began in 2015 on security issues. Until now, Komeito has been known for being the party promoting social welfare and education, but not as the main decision maker on security policies. However, since last year, they have become decision makers and their influence on the mainstay of the state is intensifying. It is important not to underestimate this development.

To my understanding, Komeito is a political party of "existential pacifists." In other words, Komeito was established to create peace and exists to preserve it. And they individual self-defense overlap. This makes it difficult to gradually broaden the interpretation of the right to individual self-defense in order to engage in activities that would significantly breach the boundaries of the right of collective self-defense.

Moreover, the question of the revision of Article 9 of the Constitution was removed, since this didn't affect activities necessary for the legitimate defense of Japan.

Meanwhile, this legislation leaves room for various interpretations, depending on one's outlook. Therefore, it's vital that this not end with the adoption of the legislation but that efforts be made in the application of the legislation to protect the spirit of the 2015 cabinet decision.

——What should be noted with regard to the application of the legislation?

Sato: For instance, when the current government was leaning toward conducting minesweeping activities in the Strait of Hormuz, it was Komeito Chief Representative Natsuo Yamaguchi's interpellation on September 14, 2015 which extracted the response that doing so would be unrealistic. It is not in the normal course of things to have rash decisions on the part of government questioned and corrected by a member of the ruling coalition. However, in order to maintain peace in

Foreword

The Komeito ("clean government") party most certainly plays a vital role in Japanese politics. As of December 10, 2016, the party holds 35 seats in the House of Representatives (7% of the total 475 seats) and 25 seats in the House of Councillors (10% of the total 242 seats). The political influence that Komeito wields, however, is far greater than the proportion of seats they occupy in parliament. Similarly, within the LDP-Komeito coalition government, many policies have been drawn by Komeito's hand. One such example is Japan's peace and national security legislation enacted on September 19, 2015. Some commentators claim that Komeito betrayed its principles as a party for peace, but this is incorrect. I expressed my opinion on the matter in an interview with the *Komei Shimbun*, reproduced in part below.

——How would you evaluate the peace and security legislation?

Sato: If I were to assess the merits of Komeito's position, I would give it full marks. Komeito asserts that this legislative package that was enacted has not altered one bit the content of the cabinet decision of July 1, 2015. That decision clarified where the right of collective self-defense and the right to

CONTENTS

Foreword   6

Chapter 1   Komeito — A Deeply Driven Column   13

Chapter 2   Komeito as a Party of the Masses   27

Chapter 3   Transition to Flight   41

Chapter 4   Confronting the "Freedom of Speech" Incident   56

Chapter 5   A Key Agent in Diplomacy   65

Chapter 6   As a Party in Ruling Coalitions   80

Editor's Note: Many of the references the author introduces in this book, including titles of his own works and passages quoted from other literature, are yet to be formally available in English at the time of this writing. The English translations of these works and passages are thus tentative versions of the original Japanese and should be understood as such.

Copyright ©Masaru Sato 2017

Published in Japan in 2017
By Daisanbunmei-sha, Inc.
1-23-5 Shinjuku Shinjuku-ku, Tokyo Japan

http://www.daisanbunmei.co.jp/

Translated from the Japanese by Katapult Corporation
Cover design by Mitsutoshi Fujiwara
Page layout by Satoshi Ando

All rights reserved.
No part of this text may be reproduced, transmitted,
or stored in or introduced into any information storage and retrieval system,
in any form or by any means whether electronic or mechanical,
now known or hereinafter invented,
without the express written permission of the publisher.

ISBN978-4-476-03360-1

Printed and Bound by TOSHO Printing Co., Ltd.

A Transformative Force
The Emergence of Komeito as a Driver of Japanese Politics

Masaru Sato

Daisanbunmei-sha

【著者略歴】
佐藤 優（さとう・まさる）
1960年、東京都生まれ。同志社大学大学院神学研究科修了後、専門職員として外務省に入省。在ロシア日本大使館に勤務し、主任分析官として活躍。2002年、背任と偽計業務妨害容疑で逮捕、起訴され、09年6月執行猶予付有罪確定。13年6月執行猶予満了。著書に、大宅壮一ノンフィクション賞を受賞した『自壊する帝国』、毎日出版文化賞特別賞を受賞した『国家の罠』、『創価学会と平和主義』（朝日新書）、『創価学会を語る』（松岡幹夫との共著／第三文明社）、『大国の掟』（NHK出版新書）、『世界観』（小学館新書）など多数。第10回安吾賞受賞。

About the Author

Masaru Sato was born in 1960 in Tokyo Prefecture. After graduating with a Master's Degree from Doshisha University Graduate School of Theology, he was hired as an officer in the Ministry of Foreign Affairs. He also served as senior analyst at the Embassy of Japan in Russia. In 2002, he was charged with malpractice and tortious obstruction. In June 2009, he was handed a probationary sentence, which was completed in June 2013.

He has authored numerous works, including "Self-destructing Empire," (Shinchosha, 2006), which won the Soichi Oya Non-fiction Prize, and "Trappings of National Power," (Shinchosha, 2007), which was awarded the Mainichi Publishing Special Culture Prize. He also wrote "Soka Gakkai and Pacifism," (Asahi Shinsho, 2014) and "Discussing the Soka Gakkai," which he co-wrote with Mikio Matsuoka, (Daisanbunmei-sha, 2015). He is the recipient of the 10th Ango Award. *A Tranceformative Force: The Emergence of Komeito as a Driver of Japanese Politics* is his first work to be published in English.

装　幀／藤原光寿
帯写真（著者）／柴田　篤
本文レイアウト／安藤　聡
写真提供（P17、P57、P96、P121、カバー、帯）／公明党機関紙委員会
英語翻訳／カタプルト コーポレーション

佐藤優の「公明党」論
2017年3月16日　初版第1刷発行

著　者	佐藤　優
発行者	大島光明
発行所	株式会社　第三文明社
	東京都新宿区新宿1-23-5
	郵便番号　160-0022
	電話番号　03-5269-7144（営業代表）
	03-5269-7145（注文専用）
	03-5269-7154（編集代表）
	振替口座　00150-3-117823
	ＵＲＬ　http://www.daisanbunmei.co.jp

印刷・製本　図書印刷株式会社

©SATO Masaru 2017　　　　　　　　　　　　　Printed in Japan
ISBN 978-4-476-03360-1
落丁・乱丁本はお取り換えいたします。ご面倒ですが、小社営業部宛お送りください。
送料は当方で負担いたします。
法律で認められた場合を除き、本書の無断複写・複製・転載を禁じます。